A Matter of Honour

And Other Tales of
Early Perth

SUSAN CODE

Published by

GENERAL STORE
PUBLISHING HOUSE

1 Main Street, Burnstown, Ontario, Canada K0J 1G0
Telephone 1-800-465-6072 Fax 613-432-7184

ISBN 1-896182-27-5
Printed and bound in Canada

Layout and Design by Leanne Enright
Cover Concept by Linda Henderson

General Store Publishing House gratefully acknowledges the assistance of the Ontario Arts Council and Canada Council.

Canadian Cataloguing in Publication Data

Code, Susan Elizabeth, 1960-
    A matter of honour: and other tales of early Perth

Includes bibliographical references and index.
ISBN 1-896182-27-5

    1. Perth (Ont.)--History, Military. 2. Perth (Ont.)--
History. I. Title

FC3099.P47C63 1996   971.3'82   C96-900270-X
F1059.5.P39C63 1996

First Printing April 1996

ACKNOWLEDGEMENTS

Writing and publishing a book are extraordinary and contradictory experiences with the same goal—to create a story that other people will want to read. The process can be quite daunting and emotionally charged. What begins as an intensely personal and private pastime is eventually exposed to the scrutiny, input and manipulation of others who claim to have only your best interests at heart. It's a bit like raising a child. As this has been my "first," I have gone through all the classic stages. I was overly protective of its early development, then cautiously accepting of outside aid as I became more confident in my abilities and am now extremely grateful to the many people who helped me bring to maturity a book to which I am very proud to sign my name.

Specifically, I would like to thank Doug McNichol and Debbie Sproule of the Perth Museum who gave me access to precious archival material and a stimulating place to conduct much of my research; Ann McPhail, librarian at the Perth Campus of Algonquin College, who presides over a marvellous collection relating to Lanark County's history; John Stevens, my editor, who gently helped me nurture my stories; and Tim Gordon, General Store publisher, who by publishing this and other Ottawa Valley books is helping to preserve this unique corner of Canada.

And, finally, I'd like to thank my family who have always had faith in me.

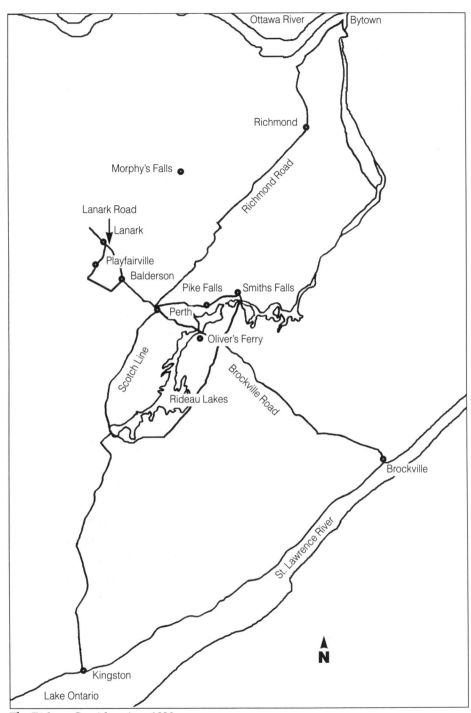

The Rideau Corridor circa 1830.

TABLE OF CONTENTS

INTRODUCTION

On Christmas Eve 1814, the Treaty of Ghent was signed ending the War of 1812 between Great Britain and the United States of America. Nothing much had been achieved by this war; all gains and losses of territory were revoked and a status quo ante-bellum imposed. However, the vulnerability of the British colonies in North America had been made glaringly obvious. It was time to put in place a comprehensive defensive plan for when the Americans attacked again. The Duke of Wellington, after his miraculous victory at the Battle of Waterloo, was charged with this commission.

Included in this scheme were extensive fortifications at Kingston, an inland water route connecting Montreal and Kingston for the safe movement of troops behind the border, and permanent military settlements populated by trained, fighting forces which could be quickly mustered in the event of war. Perth was the first of three such military settlements established in the Rideau Corridor.

In April 1816, the first military surveyors arrived and set up camp on the south side of the Tay River, across from two large islands, and proceeded to lay out a town of one mile square in the middle of untouched wilderness. They felled an immense elm tree to bridge the Tay and connect Gore Street, which eventually became the main street of Perth.

Within six months, there were 840 men, 207 women and 458 children living in the Perth Military Settlement. Eight hundred bushels of fall wheat sprouted in the rough-cleared fields, eighty head of cattle stood grazing amongst the stumps and trees, and 250 habitations sprang up in the village and immediate vicinity. Settlers consisted of disbanded soldiers and half-pay officers from several regiments who had fought both in Europe and North America, including two from Switzerland, the De Meuron and De Watteville Regiments. They received land grants, commensurate in size with their ranks, which discouraged them from returning home and causing havoc in a country, now at peace, with too many people and not enough jobs. The British government also provided financial assistance to civilians, encouraging them to emigrate to Perth thus helping to relieve the overcrowded parishes. The first to take up this offer came from the Glasgow area and brought with them the many Scottish place names which now grace the countryside.

This "instant" community is an oddity in Canadian settlement history. The large numbers of moneyed and educated settlers— younger sons of good families—meant that fine stone homes were built in the first generation, not the second, standards were maintained no matter what the circumstances, and being a small, isolated community was not considered a stumbling block when trying to develop the town and influence provincial and national affairs.

In the Perth Military Settlement, where one in five of the original settlers was a half-pay officer and veteran of the War of 1812, rank meant everything. A middling lieutenant at the Battle of Ogdensburg, with persistence and connections, could aspire to a majority or even colonelcy in the militia. If successful, he could then secure for himself one or more of the profitable government appointments so necessary for developing a new country.

These realities often led to some bizarre incidents.

The stories in this collection are both true and factual, although the manner of telling them is strictly my own. There is no need to make anything up when your history is as fantastic as Perth's, although occasionally I did have to draw some of my own conclusions.

I found my richest source for details in the diaries of the Reverend William Bell. A Scotsman, moralist and keen observer, the Reverend Bell arrived in Perth in 1817 as the settlement's first minister and lived here until his death in 1857.

For public versions of events, I scoured early copies of the *Brockville Recorder*, the *Bathurst Independent Examiner* and the *Bathurst Courier*, predecessor of today's *Perth Courier*, the second oldest weekly newspaper in Canada still publishing. I also made good use of the archives at the Perth Campus of Algonquin College and the Perth Museum where I was able to dip into historical records and contemporary reports, such as Robert Gourlay's controversial *Statistical Account of Upper Canada*, published in 1822. I relied heavily on the research of several local historians whose chronicles have preceded my own minor effort at keeping the light of Perth's rich past still burning. Believe me, my copies of your works are all well thumbed, and I strongly suggest to those of you who wish to learn more about Perth and this era to read these books. They're listed in the attached bibliography.

But, most of all, I was raised on these stories. My father's family—Wexford Irish, who weren't going to let some Lowland Scots beat them out on a good thing—settled here around 1819 and managed to eke out a living by fair means . . . mostly. But that's another story for another time.

Susan Code

Perth, 1828. This watercolour, by Rideau Canal Clerk of Works Thomas Burrowes, was painted from the north-east bank of the Tay River on Gore Street and it depicts the town twelve years after its founding as a military settlement in 1816. Cockburn Island sits in the foreground, while on top of the hill to the left are the Roman Catholic church, the Summit House, the Anglican church (both churches subsequently burned down and have been replaced) and the original courthouse and gaol, which was built of brick. Coming down the hill to the right on Craig Street, the only substantial building is Adamson's Inn, renamed the Red House by the Duke of Richmond in 1819. *Credit: Archives of Ontario.*

THE SNUB

A blanket of fresh snow covered the small collection of buildings that huddled around two islands frozen in the Tay River. Thin wisps of grey smoke shivered from the chimneys, and a sallow sun tried vainly to spark a glimmer from the icicles that picketed each home. A door slammed and a dog yelped. The jingle of sleigh-bells cracked the wintry stillness, and joyous laughter pealed out behind the horses as they raced through the deserted streets, barely noticing the small party trudging out the Brockville Road. With a sniff of his long nose, the Reverend William Bell twitched his curtains shut on the unseemly conduct and returned to scratching out his sermon on One's Duty to Suppress Disorder by Setting a Good Example.

The Yuletide had long been swept away, but some unpleasant after-effects had managed to roll over into the new year of 1833. Of course there were the usual complaints—too rich food, too much drink and too many relatives in too small a house—but all of them had been forgotten in the warm afterglow of a joyous season spent with good friends and cheer. Except for one.

Love has a funny habit of disturbing the natural order of things. It blinds some men to their ambitions and others to their prejudices. And so it happened when Alexander McMillan, veteran of the Battle of Chrysler's Farm, first registrar for Lanark and Renfrew, government land agent in North Lanark, Justice of the Peace, director of the Tay Navigation Company and lieutenant-colonel of the First Lanark Militia Regiment, fell prey to Cupid's arrow and married his servant girl.

11

This was simply not done in class-conscious Perth.

It was alright to bed the girl, inconvenient to get her pregnant, but by no means did a gentleman have to make an honest woman of the impertinent creature. This, Donald Fraser, McMillan's successful opponent at the polls the previous spring, had learned from his family when he tried to wed the servant girl he had put in a family way. Such a *mésalliance* would prove harmful to his promising political career, not to mention the ostracism they would suffer in polite society.

Well, Colonel McMillan, despondent from his electoral defeat, threw caution to the winds and married his heart's desire. It caused quite a to-do, as you can imagine, throughout the town of Perth.

Now when a man marries hastily or unwisely, his friends and neighbours often perform a charivari for the new couple. Fortified with drums, horns and plenty of drink, the raucous gang will descend on the honeymooners in disguise and will not leave until rewarded with refreshments and money. On one occasion in Perth:

> (the) one who acted as spokesman had a woman's cap on his head, a pillow on his belly to make him look a woman with child, a burden on his back to give him the appearance of a beggar-wife, and an old bed cover over his shoulders . . . Some of the party had their faces blackened and four or five wore masks some of which were ugly enough. One of them consisted of a whole headpiece like a helmut (sic), the face painted in a frightful manner and the forehead furnished with two lofty horns which gave to the whole a very unpleasant aspect . . . (Another wore) a buffalo skin with the hairy side out, and had a string of horsebells round his neck.[1]

So, on the two evenings following the McMillan nuptials, a party tried to get up a charivari, but "the performers could neither muster up numbers nor courage enough to come up to the house. A report had gone abroad that the Colonel had threatened to shoot the first that came. This, however, was so far from the case that he had provided a supper for them."[2]

Poor Colonel and Mrs McMillan.

[1] Rev. Wm. Bell Diaries.
[2] Ibid. 3 April 1832.

However, despite the failed charivari, many were still eager to pass comment on the new bride. On the Sunday following their wedding day, a gaggle of gossips gathered on the steps of the court-house to cast a jaundiced eye over Mrs McMillan as she attended services next door at St James'. They went home disappointed. It turned out that as Mrs McMillan had no new finery that befitted her elevated station in life, and as no one but the drummer and his wife had come to call on them in the meantime, she was ashamed to show her face.

Maybe the Colonel should not have been so hasty in giving his silk hat to the minister who married them. This parson had truly answered a higher calling and objected to taking money for performing the ceremony. He likened it to selling the privileges of the gospel, but he would accept presents.

Well, things did not improve for the star-crossed lovers. Accepted by neither the soldier nor officer classes, Mrs McMillan suffered the cold shoulder of an insular community. There were whispers in the shops, slights on the street and omissions from the guest lists, until Colonel McMillan could take it no more. When Dr and Mrs Thom hosted an evening to celebrate the Christmas season and invited the Colonel but not his wife, McMillan challenged Thom to a duel.

Dr Alexander Thom, staff surgeon to the Perth Military Settlement, was one of the richest men in this half-pay officers' paradise. Commissioned as surgeon with the 41st Regiment (Second Somersetshires) in 1799, by 1813, he was in Canada as one of nine staff surgeons with the British Army's Medical Department of War. He was not a nice man. More concerned with his many industrial and land-development interests, the Reverend Bell accused him of often neglecting his medical duties:

> Dr Thom received a salary from the government for attending the sick, yet he often treated them with the greatest brutality.[3]

He had even tried to keep prices for quinine up during the cholera epidemic that swept through the Canadas like an avenging mistress the previous summer of 1832.

In addition to owning the first saw and grist mill in Perth and developing its first subdivision, Caroline Village, on part of his

[3] Rev. Wm. Bell Diaries.

800-acre land grant, Dr Thom—like Colonel McMillan—was also a Justice of the Peace and a frustrated politician. By January 1833, Dr Thom had run three times for the Legislative Assembly in York—and had lost three times.

Now in order for a duel to be considered official, the combatants must have seconds to ensure that all is conducted fairly. They must also be prepared to see the duel through to its natural end if either principal fails to honour the challenge. In this, McMillan and Thom were ably served by Thomas Radenhurst and Francis Cumming respectively.

Thomas Radenhurst was one of Perth's first lawyers, coming to the settlement in 1824. Although a great champion of Reform, he had been educated by the eminent Tory, Bishop Strachan, and was married to the daughter of Thomas Ridout, surveyor-general of Upper Canada and a member of the Family Compact. He was recognized for his strict integrity and professional pursuits despite his volatile temper. He had engaged in public fisticuffs with another Perth lawyer, James Boulton, on at least one occasion and knew about duelling first-hand. Thomas Radenhurst and James Boulton once rowed across the border to an island in the St Lawrence River to engage in a duel with pistols. Both survived without a scratch.

Francis Cumming was also a half-pay officer and a captain in the First Regiment of the Lanark Militia. Colonel McMillan was his superior officer, which must have made for some interesting times in the officers' mess afterwards. Since leaving the army, Cumming had had a rather unsuccessful career in journalism. In 1828, he founded the *Brockville Gazette*, which he left in 1830 to come to Perth and take over the *Bathurst Independent Examiner*. This newspaper had been an unprofitable venture since its inception and finally succumbed under Cumming's editorship, not long before this honourable engagement. Cumming had gladly sold the printing press to William Tully, who was trying to make a go with a new weekly, the *Perth Constitution*.

So, on Friday, the fourth day of January, eighteen hundred and thirty-three, two grown men faced each other across a white counterpane of snow. Pistols raised, each bristled with indignation to the point that neither could hold his weapon steady.

It was an outrage! Honour was at stake. A man's wife had been slighted. And so it had come to this. Pistols. On the Brockville Road. In that time-honoured method of Resolving Matters of Honour Between Gentlemen. A duel.

Barely controlling their fury at the insults that had been exchanged, the two middle-aged soldiers paced off, turned, and fired.

Dr Thom fell.

The attending doctor ran to his fallen colleague to determine the extent of his injuries. The two seconds quickly conferred and declared that honour had been satisfied. The principals, too, amicably agreed that the matter had been suitably resolved and set about to repair to their homes. The attending doctor could find nothing more serious than a bruise on Dr Thom's leg, so with a few strong arms to offer the fallen man assistance, the small party proceeded apace.

The new *Perth Constitution* dutifully reported this exciting event and received some provincial renown when other papers picked up the item, including the *Brockville Recorder:*

The Perth Constitution of the 12th inst. has the following paragraph: DUEL—On Friday last, Alexander McMillan, Esq. and Alexander Thom, Esquire, met in a field on the Brockville road, to decide an affair of honour—the former attended by Mr. Radenhurst, and the latter by Mr. Cumming. After exchanging shots, the seconds interfered, and on mutual explanations being made, the matter terminated amicably. Dr. Thom received a contusion on the leg.[4]

Honour is, indeed, everything.

---

[4] *Brockville Recorder*, 17 January 1833.

THE PETTY DESPOT

Daniel Daverne sat at his desk figuring accounts. The magistrate was due that afternoon to conduct his quarterly inspection of the books, and everything had to be in order. As secretary to the still-quite-new Perth Military Settlement, he oversaw every single detail involved in establishing the community, from assigning lots and issuing monthly stores to new settlers, to maintaining the settlement's accounts and conducting correspondence with headquarters in Quebec. There was nothing that went on in Perth that he did not influence or control.

The door opened and an austere figure dressed in black crossed the threshold and positioned himself firmly before Daverne. Disapproval and contained anger permeated every corner of the room, but still Daverne kept scratching away at his ledger, apparently oblivious to the change in atmosphere.

"Where's m'stove, Daverne."

The secretary turned away in search of some missing documentation.

"His Excellency approved a stove for the school some months past, and I have yet to see any sign of it. Winter is coming, mon, and I'll brook no further delay in the delivery of m'stove." Reverend William Bell's voice rose with his last words to a pitch normally reserved for his more admonitory sermons. It was impossible for Daverne to continue ignoring his presence.

"Stove, what stove, Mr Bell?"

"No more of your dithering, Daverne! First you couldn't find the order. Another time you said you had to write to your superior, Captain Fowler, and yet another time you told me that I might have my stove if I sent to Fort Wellington for it. No more will you put me off."

"Mr Bell," Daverne began coldly, "you have been granted a generous annual salary of fifty pounds sterling for your meagre efforts as schoolmaster to the miserable urchins of this settlement. Which I, a poor civil servant earning a paltry ten shillings—*Army* sterling—a day for unceasing toil in the king's service, consider far too generous. So, since you enjoy such princely standing with the governor, I suggest that you write to him directly for your precious stove. That is, if you want it so badly and are not prepared to pay for it yourself. I have no time for frivolous requests from odious hangers-on such as yourself. Good day, sir."

"Never," Bell sputtered, "never in all my born days have I ever had the misfortune to encounter a person of so malignant a disposition as yourself. It is with pleasure that I take my request to the governor."

Daverne mentally shrugged his indifference as the reverend swept out in high indignation. He flipped back a few pages in his ledger and noted with satisfaction the price he had received for the sale of one stove. What did he care if that pious raven wrote to the governor and croaked about the continued absence of a single stove. The governor was in Quebec, at least a week's journey away. All stores came from the Lower Province and there were more than enough opportunities for one stove, and many other items, to go astray. No one would inquire too deeply as to where the first stove went, if the Quarter-Master's Department decided to issue Bell another. As long as he kept filing his quarterly reports, duly notarized and on time, no one would ever think to look too closely at him for answers. Besides, he could bring down too many people in his wake.

Daverne was brought back to attention by the arrival of Francis Cumming, one of the magistrates of the Perth Military Settlement authorized to inspect its books. The secretary liked to dispense with this ritual as quickly as possible and usually managed to occupy most of the presiding magistrate's time with questions on his various entrepreneurial concerns. As well as being an effective ploy, this often yielded useful information. Eventually, the magistrate would recall the reason for his presence and then ask Daverne to swear to the correctness of his returns; he would do so, his hand placed solemnly on a French dictionary.

For it all depended on which ledger was examined, and your point of view, as to whether or not the figures were correct.

It was too easy.

Daverne accompanied Cumming to the door and waved him on his way, with just the right mix of servitude and command. He paused to take in the bustle of industry before him. Although it had been barely three years since the first settlers arrived here in the spring of 1816, a full grid of streets had already been surveyed by Reuben Sherwood creating an "instant" town of one mile square straddling the Tay River. It had several bakers, smiths, stores, breweries, mills and a post office, and new settlers were coming in on a steady stream.

He closed the door on the busy town and the woman who spat an epithet in his direction. He gave little thought to the ordinary settlers, seeing them only as a means to his own advancement. Their futures in the settlement were his to command, and he wasted no time in taking advantage of their weaknesses and ignorance. By the time they reached Perth, they were exhausted and completely overwhelmed with the enormity of the step they had taken. First there were six weeks tossing across the North Atlantic in the cramped hold of a tiny sailing ship, then a few days' breather in the rough-and-tumble port city of Montreal, before finally undergoing the 200-mile tow, portage and walk to Perth through uncut wilderness. If the mosquitoes didn't cut them down to size, the extent of this wild land did. Most of these Scots and Irish—mostly Irish, like himself—had never before been further than the next well-cultivated parish and had never owned more than the clothes on their backs. They were here now, finally, ready to claim their hundred acres and a chance at a real future. But not without a little fun for Daniel Daverne first.

Much of the land surrounding the Perth Military Settlement was marginal at best; there were many surveyed lots that just could not be cultivated by a single hand, due to flooding, rocks and cedars growing so thickly they matted together to form a near-impenetrable wall. A settler, having discovered he'd been assigned a lot like this, could ask to exchange it for another one. Now by rights, Daverne should have taken this information and marked the maps accordingly, but that would have robbed him of any pleasure in this backwoods pimple. What was the use of being in charge if he couldn't also be in control? So, time after time, he sent settler after settler to inspect the same worthless lots. The wretches could be wandering for days looking for their promised land.

Eventually, he would relent and direct them to a suitable area. But he could still twitch their obeisance back to him when he felt the need. As part of the contract of settlement, the government promised each adult man granted a lot rations, axes, ploughs and other necessary implements for establishing a homestead. Daverne, however, often found some reason why he couldn't fulfil this promise and would send the settler away to make the long walk home, footsore, empty-handed and wondering how he would provide for his family in this hostile land.

Settlers, once given a location ticket, were required to clear a certain number of acres in three years, and bring them under cultivation, before they were given clear title to the property. Men who had been skilled craftsmen in Scotland and Ireland often found that they made more progress if they hired an able axeman to clear their land, leaving them free to ply their trade and earn some valuable cash. Daverne, getting wind of this, would then suspend their rations on the technicality that the ticket holder was no longer working his land, even though the work was still being done.

And then, when the land was finally cleared, Daverne would find all sorts of bureaucratic excuses as to why he could not issue a clear title.

They could rant and rave, and write as many letters as they liked to the governor, the Quarter-Master General and even the British newspapers, for that matter, but, Daverne reminded himself, as long as he was in Perth and the powers that be were elsewhere, there was very little that anyone could do. He was in control. He had the power to squash anyone who caused trouble for him in Quebec. And he used it gladly.

Bell, however, was a particularly bothersome insect. He was always droning on about some injustice or other and was not as easy to brush away as the other midges in the settlement. But Daverne had managed to distract him somewhat by engineering the arrival of the Reverend Michael Harris to minister on behalf of the established Church of England. Daverne laughed at the hornets' nest he'd created here. The two men disliked each other intensely on every level, practically on sight, and Daverne had been able to sit back and watch, with wicked amusement, the battle between kirk and church, Scot and Irish. He had masterfully set Bell up against Harris by soliciting his signature on a petition for an Episcopal clergyman, on the rationale that there was currently no one in the settlement who could perform baptisms or administer Communion.

This, of course, was a complete fallacy, but the Calvinist Bell would administer solely to the devout, and most in the military settlement subscribed only to be "wedded, bedded and dead-ed," much to Bell's constant disapproval. The Reverend Harris was a bit more forgiving than his intractable colleague.

Spring soon turned into summer, and life in the Perth Military Settlement continued along its now established pattern. Buildings grew, a few more stubborn acres were cleared, and Daniel Daverne grew more tyrannical, overbearing and despised each day.

Then, one warm day in July, Colonel Francis Cockburn, Deputy Quarter-Master General to the Forces, arrived in Perth. He had come from headquarters in Quebec to inspect the Rideau military settlements for which he was ultimately responsible. Daverne was not happy to see his superior and worked hard at keeping a neutral countenance while he stood watching the colonel making himself at home in the office of the military stores.

"Daverne," began the colonel, as he casually flipped through the ledger, "I am not pleased to see you and I think you know why."

Daverne remained silent.

"What started as an occasional trickle, which could easily be wiped away, has turned into an absolute torrent of complaints about your brutal behaviour towards the inhabitants of this place. On the road from the Richmond Military Settlement, I met a great number of men who spared no breath telling me of your ruthless conduct. How did that man describe you?" Cockburn paused and looked up from the ledger while he appeared to search his mind. "Oh, yes," and he looked straight into Daverne's still-inscrutable face. "'Never have I met with a person of so malignant a disposition.'" Cockburn was all military command now.

"You have brought undue, unfavourable attention to yourself, Daverne. I didn't expect you to win any popularity contests out here, but I did think you would know how to control your greed. I am now going to have to give serious consideration to the complaints that a deputation of upstanding men is about to present to me any . . . Ah, I see them coming up the street now. We'll continue this conversation later. In the meantime, you can give some thought as to how we can contain this mess."

Colonel Cockburn spent the next hour listening to the litany of grievances against the settlement's secretary. When they had finally finished, he bridged his fingers over his nose, thanked the gentlemen present for their concern, and promised to give all their charges the serious attention they deserved. As the party prepared to leave, Colonel Cockburn asked the Reverend William Bell, Doctor Alexander Thom, Commissary General Joshua Adams and Captains McMillan and Marshall to stay behind.

"Gentlemen," he began, "it is obvious that a thorough investigation into the conduct of Daniel Daverne is necessary, and I would like you to serve as the Board of Inquiry. You are all respected men of this settlement, and I trust you to examine the evidence with impartiality. You can rest assured that if Daverne is found guilty, he will be discharged in disgrace, and I know that I can rely on you to put aside your personal differences and give him your unconditional support should he be found innocent. Now, I don't see any reason to delay the proceedings . . ."

"Colonel Cockburn."

"Yes, Mr Bell?"

"Sir, with all due respect, I request that I be excused from this office due to my profession, as one of the Lord's ministers, and the number of complaints I personally have against Mr Daverne."

"Nonsense, Reverend," objected the colonel. "While I appreciate your concerns, it is precisely because of your position in this community that I want you, like your peers here, to serve on this board. You must be as well, if not better, acquainted with Mr Daverne's conduct, and so I must beg you to reconsider."

Reverend Bell seemed to accept Colonel Cockburn's assurances and, there being no other objections, the investigation began at once. Colonel Cockburn ordered the clerks to bring forth the settlement's records, and everyone set to work.

The clerks were kept busy throughout the day searching out papers and books as question after question was raised concerning the administration of the Perth Military Settlement. Soon, the enormity and extent of the crimes that Daverne had perpetrated against the settlers and the Quarter-Master's Department were apparent to all. Bell's much delayed stove was merely a drop in a bucket overflowing with misappropriations. Discrepancies showed that Daverne had been embezzling government stores to a large amount. He had also been lining his own pockets by filing false returns with Quebec. Magistrates Thom, McMillan and Marshall squirmed uneasily when they realized that Daverne had sworn his oaths as to the veracity of his accounts on a French dictionary.

Eight hours later, Colonel Cockburn ran his hands over his face and through his hair, stood up and went to look out the window at the setting sun.

"Gentlemen," he said, fatigue hanging from the single word, "it is getting late. I think it is safe to say that we are all profoundly shocked at what has been brought to light today. It is also Saturday evening, and I would dearly like to go to the inn for a drink.

"So, shall we remove ourselves there for some much needed reflection and resume our inquiry tomorrow morning?" proposed Cockburn.

"Ahem," interjected Bell piously. "May I remind you that tomorrow is the sabbath and, as such, should be devoted to religious purposes. I, of course, have services to conduct and cannot attend, but even if I did not, for us to engage in temporal matters on the sabbath is not only a sin against God, but it would set a bad example before the settlers."

"Forgive me, Mr Bell," apologized Cockburn. "You are right, of course. We will all attend divine worship tomorrow and reconvene on Monday morning. Now, to Adamson's Inn."

The members of the Board of Inquiry gathered up their belongings and gratefully exited the stuffy room. Colonel

Cockburn stopped, closed his eyes and breathed in the freshness of the soft summer breeze that drifted gently down the Tay. When he opened his eyes, he saw Bell standing determinedly before him.

"Have we not done enough today, Mr Bell? Or, at least, can't it wait until we've slaked our thirst?"

"As I do not approve of strong drink, I shall not be accompanying you,"—this came as no surprise to Cockburn—"but I would like to suggest that one more task be done before nightfall."

Cockburn raised a questioning eyebrow. Bell took this sign as permission to continue.

"In light of what we have learned today, and the speed news travels in this settlement, do you not think it likely that Daverne will make his escape? The evidence against him is too damning, and we cannot afford to wait until the inquiry resumes on Monday before taking appropriate action. A warrant for his arrest should be obtained without delay."

For just a heartbeat, Cockburn paled, and then a slow smile relaxed across his features.

"Come now, Mr Bell. It is true that Mr Daverne appears guilty of many serious charges, but why would he flee? As we saw, he owns a great deal of property in the settlement, too much, in fact, to run away and leave it. Don't you agree McMillan?"

The magistrate, who had waited with the others to escort Cockburn, started at being singled out.

"Well, sir. There are certain issues to consider. I mean . . . What I am trying to say . . . We mustn't forget . . ."

"Mr Bell," Cockburn began lightly, "while I appreciate your concerns, I think you are overreacting. Look, so sure am I of Daverne's ties to this settlement, I will wager anyone present here a dozen of wine that he will not attempt to escape. The man is a gentleman serving in His Majesty's army. It would not be the honourable thing to do."

And with that, Cockburn dismissed the matter and cheerfully told McMillan to lead on.

The sabbath rose fine and clear, and Reverend Bell welcomed a large congregation to his first service in First Presbyterian, the new church at the corner of Drummond and Halton streets. No more would he have to conduct divine services in Adamson's Inn. Most of the officers in Perth and many of the settlers were present, and Colonel Cockburn hurried in to take his seat just as the clock struck eleven. Reverend Bell had seen him coming from the direction of the military stores and frowned his disapproval at the Deputy Quarter-Master General, which Cockburn duly ignored.

On Monday morning, the Board of Inquiry reconvened. Colonel Cockburn was the last to take his seat.

"Gentlemen," he began briskly, "some new developments have occurred since we adjourned on Saturday night."

Bell was distracted by the frantic actions of the clerks in the other room and almost missed Cockburn's next words.

". . . Kingston to await the pleasure of the Governor-General."

"I beg your pardon, Colonel Cockburn, who has gone to Kingston?" asked Bell at the same time as one of the agitated clerks rushed into the room and whispered something in Cockburn's ear.

"What?" Cockburn roared.

"What is going on?" Bell asked Captain Marshall. "Who has gone to Kingston?"

"Daverne," replied Marshall. "On the colonel's orders."

"Colonel Cockburn," Bell turned indignantly to the Quarter-Master who was following the clerk out of the room. "What is the meaning of this action?"

"Not now, Bell. It appears that Daverne has taken all of the coin belonging to the Perth Military Settlement."

A young soldier, short of breath from running, burst into the military stores.

"He's gone," he panted.

"Who's gone?" asked Dr. Thom.

"Daverne," gasped the soldier. "We were to escort him to Kingston, where the Duke of Richmond is soon expected. But when we got to his quarters, he was gone. Must've left sometime during the night."

All of a sudden, everyone was talking at once, demanding answers and hurling accusations. Pandemonium reigned as the enormity of the situation became apparent. Daniel Daverne, secretary to the Perth Military Settlement and its most despised and feared resident, had flown, taking with him whatever he hadn't already stolen.

∽

Colonel Cockburn immediately dissolved the Board of Inquiry, much to Reverend Bell's disapproval. Whispers circulated that any further investigation would have embarrassed officials higher up, but no one could say for sure.

Major James Powell, as senior officer in the settlement, was appointed superintendent and charged with saving the community from collapse. But this quick action did not stop the stories of corruption that flowed freely for years throughout both provinces, discouraging immigrants from settling in Perth.

Daverne, meanwhile, had headed straight to Brockville, where he managed to get across the St Lawrence before his disgrace became widely known. One of his victims eventually caught up with him in Utica, New York, had him arrested and then made him pay back the money stolen from him. After his release, Daverne went to stay with a cousin living in New York. He returned this cousin's kindness by seducing and carrying off his wife to Albany, where he continued to practise his evil ways. He wasn't as lucky here, however, and was severely beaten by some of his dupes before he could get out of town.

Daverne eventually made his way back to Canada to a farm near Kingston he had purchased some years previously for his father. There he set up a whisky distillery, which he ran until his death not long afterwards. He died detested by all who knew him.

The final word must go to the Reverend Bell, who derived great satisfaction in Daverne's eventual downfall.

The fate of this man shows how true it is that honesty is the best policy, and that the triumphing of the wicked is short . . . For verily there is a God that ruleth in the earth; who setteth up one and putteth down another as he sees fit. The curse of the Lord is in the house of the wicked, but he blesseth the habitation of the just![1]

---

[1] Diaries of the Rev. Wm. Bell, 1819

The Reverend William Bell (1780-1857) as photographed in 1848. Rev. Bell arrived in Perth from Scotland in 1817 as the settlement's first minister and second schoolteacher. A tireless missionary, in his first seven years he travelled 4,000 miles–mostly on foot–and preached 900 sermons. Bell had been a building contractor in London before entering the ministry and emigrating, and was well-suited to the rough life of Upper Canada. He passed on his experiences and advice to prospective settlers in his very popular guide *Hints to Emigrants,* which was published in Scotland in 1824.
Credit: Perth Museum.

The Reverend Michael Harris, an Irishman, was ordained a Church of England priest in 1819 at Quebec by Bishop Mountain and appointed directly to Perth, at that time a mission of the Society for the Propagation of the Gospel in Foreign Parts. Like his colleague and antagonist, Reverend Bell, Harris spent his entire career in Perth, where he died in 1856.
Credit: Perth Museum.

AN IGNOBLE END

There was a sound of revelry by night,
And Belgium's capital had gathered then
Her Beauty and her Chivalry, and bright
The lamps shone o'er fair women and brave men;
A thousand hearts beat happily; and when
Music arose with its voluptuous swell,
Soft eyes looked love to eyes which spake again,
And all went merry as a marriage bell—
But hush! hark! a deep sound strikes like a rising knell!

Or the car rattling o'er the stony street;
On with the dance! let joy be unconfined;
No sleep till morn, when Youth and Pleasure meet
To chase the glowing Hours with flying feet—
But hark!—that heavy sound breaks in once more,
As if the clouds its echo would repeat;
Arm! Arm! it is—it is—the cannon's opening roar!

The narrator had reached the climax of Byron's masterpiece, and forty wine glasses rose also in acknowledgment of the great poet's tribute to the Duchess of Richmond's famous ball on the eve of the Battle of Waterloo. For here, in the upper room of Adamson's Inn, was Childe Harold himself (at least for tonight) - Charles Lennox, direct descendant of Charles II and his mistress Louise de Kiroualle, one-time member of the British House of Commons, former Lord Lieutenant of Ireland, Governor-in-Chief of British North America—the Duke of Richmond.

Now, Captain Adamson's inn was a far cry from the Duchess' Brussels ballroom, but the sturdy, two-storey oak structure was the finest and largest building the three-year-old Perth Military Settlement had to offer. In addition to receiving travellers to this isolated British outpost, Adamson's Inn also served the community as church, school, Masonic Hall and meeting room, as the occasion demanded. The upstairs gallery, generously dubbed a ballroom on this sultry August evening, had a hinged partition which could be lowered or raised and fastened to the ceiling by an iron hook, depending on the size of the gathering.

And on this evening, the gathering was large. Major John Powell, newly appointed secretary and superintendent of the Perth Military Settlement, was host, and every man of importance in Perth had paid the twenty-eight shillings for the privilege of dining with His Grace. While most were veterans of the Napoleonic Wars, and some had fought under Wellington, this was their first opportunity to have an intimate discussion with a man who had actually led a charge at Waterloo! Actually, the two dukes could trace their acquaintanceship back to the years when Richmond was Lord Lieutenant of Ireland and Wellington his subordinate.

The Duke of Richmond was extremely interested to learn the progress of the Perth Military Settlement. He had only been Governor-in-Chief of the Canadas for about a year and was determined to learn as much as he could of the colonies first-hand. Britain had achieved peace with the United States less than five years before, and it was crucial that secure defensive strategies be put in place to combat any future attacks against the Canadas by the Americans. To this end, Richmond had set out from Quebec City on the twenty-first of June, 1819 aboard the steamer *Lady Sherbrooke*. Accompanied by two of his sons, three of his daughters (the rest of his fourteen children had stayed behind in England with the duchess), and numerous attendants, he sailed first to Montreal and then to Sorel, where they rested at Fort William Henry while Colonel Francis Cockburn rushed ahead to Perth to investigate complaints about Daniel Daverne, the settlement's secretary.

Cockburn rejoined the viceregal party a few days later, in Prescott, declaring the troublesome matter had solved itself, leaving them free to spend the rest of the summer on progress throughout the upper colony going as far west as Drummond Island on Lake Huron, the most westerly military outpost. After a leisurely sojourn in York and again at Kingston, where the duke enjoyed the hospitality of the 70th Regiment playing cricket, rackets and horseback riding, the party divided, only the necessary few opting to travel the arduous overland route to Perth. The duke wished to investigate the feasibility of an inland military highway passing through Perth and linking Kingston to Nepean Point on the Ottawa River.

Land travel in Upper Canada was horrendous at best, but the duke's military years stood him in good stead as he checked out the primitive trail over rock and bog. Some attributed his ease with rough travel to the fact that he had been born in a barn— his mother caught off guard by his premature arrival.

Either way, to the great delight of everyone, the Duke of Richmond finally arrived in Perth on Saturday, the twenty-first of August, eighteen hundred-and-nineteen, and established himself at Adamson's Inn.

The duke, despite his obvious fatigue and slight tetchiness, proved a congenial guest. While draining six glasses of brandy and water, he flattered a gushing Mrs Adamson and complimented her and her husband on their fine establishment. "Although, I say," he politely suggested, "that this place would be greatly improved if it were painted red. Not only would it never need painting again, but it would give the inn the visual presence its stature demands."

Mrs Adamson thanked His Grace for his valued opinion and promised that her husband would act upon it in honour of his visit.

A delegation, headed by the Reverend William Bell, was also on hand to greet the king's representative. They presented an address to His Grace and invited the duke to be their guest of honour at a dinner the following evening. He accepted with pleasure.

The evening turned out, as promised, to be a splendid affair. One succulent dish after another came forth, borne on the scents of ever-more-tantalizing treats from Mrs Adamson's kitchens below, and the wine flowed freely, bubbling along on the stream of gossip that swirled about the room.

"To the King!"

"Do you think Mad George will ever die? I hear that he's at death's door."

"They've been saying that for thirty years."

"To the Prince Regent!"

"`Georgie, Porgie puddin' and pie, kissed the girls and made them cry . . .' What's worse—a king who barks like a dog or one that struts like a peacock but has pockets to let?"

"To the Duke of Clarence and the Navy!"

"I heard the young duchess lost her first baby in childbirth this spring."

"That old sea dog! How many children does he need? He already has ten by Mrs Jordan, the actress."

"A legitimate heir to the throne."

"To the Duke of York and the Army!"

"Did you know that Richmond challenged York to a duel? It was years ago, shortly after he entered the Coldstream Guards, which York commanded. They met with pistols on Wimbledon Common and Richmond grazed York's head!"

"No!"

"Yes! York refused to fire, even on Richmond's urging, and declared that he had only come out to give his opponent satisfaction. He never had any intention of firing on him. Both left the field with honour satisfied."

"To His Grace, the Duke of Richmond!"

"My, he's not looking well. I heard that he was bitten on his right thumb when he patted an officer's pet fox while at Sorel. But that was nearly two months ago and he has not complained of the incident since."

"Mind you, he did spend the day walking the Scotch Line, inspecting it for improvements as a road to Kingston. That would wear out even the heartiest of men."

"And he missed divine service! Much, I hear, to the Reverend Bell's disgust, too, although I see it was not enough to keep him away from this evening's festivities."

"To the Lieutenant-Governor, Sir Peregrine Maitland!"

"He's the duke's son-in-law, you know. Eloped with his daughter, Lady Sarah, in Paris, 'gainst the Duke's wishes. Hard feelings all 'round, even 'though Maitland broke Napoleon's cavalry lines at Waterloo. Wellington himself had to intervene personally. The two came out together last year to take up their respective posts, so I guess Nosey managed to get things patched up between them."

"To the Deputy Quarter-Master General, Colonel Cockburn!"

"I'm surprised that man has the gall to show his face again in this town. He's responsible, I stake my oath, for letting that scoundrel, Daverne, slip out with most of this settlement's money."

And, as the candles guttered low, casting long shadows over the carnage that was all that remained of the feast, the town fathers bestowed a final blessing on their most esteemed guest:

"That Your Grace may accomplish the rest of your journey in health and safety is our most ardent wish."

On Tuesday, the twenty-fourth of August, the duke's party left Perth to continue the journey to Nepean Point. His symptoms of illness had worsened, and he now showed a marked aversion to water. The mere pouring of water into a basin, so that he could wash, seemed to cause him great pain. Several quietly remarked that they had heard His Grace pace the floor all through the night and cautiously suggested that maybe they should delay their journey, at least until the weather relieved itself of the pressing heat and humidity. No one looked forward to the next stage of their journey to the most recently established military settlement of Richmond. It would be thirty miles over craggy hills and through mosquito-plagued swamps—all on foot.

But the duke brushed their concerns aside. Arrangements had already been made for a bateau to convey them down the Ottawa River to Montreal, where he would rejoin his family. He would brook no further delay.

With difficulty, the party reached Richmond two days later. His condition had obviously worsened. His aversion to water had become a disturbing phobia, his normally affable manner displaced by increasingly frequent ravings. However, he established himself at the Masonic Arms and informed the landlord, Major

Hill, that he wished to host a dinner the next evening for the prominent citizens of his namesake settlement. Although the duke showed obvious signs of uneasiness all evening, the dinner, like the one in Perth, was a success. In appreciation, the residents named their township after one of the duke's many titles, the Earl of March.

That night, Richmond's Swiss valet summoned Doctor Collins, a half-pay officer from the 6th Infantry, to examine his master. However, no matter how often the doctor bled him or induced his patient to gargle, the duke showed no signs of improvement.

Come morning, they made an early start by canoe down the Jock River. They hadn't travelled far before the Duke, in a fit of frenzy, leapt out of the canoe and ran into the forest, frothing at the mouth.

"Quick! After him! He's gone berserk!"

A mad scramble of aides tore after the duke into the dense underbrush. Crashing through the thick growth of virgin forest, they caught glimpses of the deranged duke as he nimbly flitted through the trees, his sightless eyes somehow showing him the way. A shaft of light cut through the trees to expose a crude barn and cabin huddled together in a small clearing. The duke followed this beacon, threw himself into the hay mow and collapsed, exhausted.

"Run to the village and get the doctors! See if there is anyone in that hut!"

The aides scattered to obey orders, frightened by the quivering, jabbering man curled up in the hay. They found that the rough farm belonged to a man named Chapman, who readily put his home at their disposal.

Doctor Collins tried bleeding him again, but to no avail. Although the duke did experience brief periods of sanity, it was obvious to all that he was dying of rabies. In a few hours, it was over.

They conveyed the body of His Grace, Charles Lennox, fourth Duke of Richmond and Lennox, in a plain deal box to the Richmond Landing where the bateau owned by Philemon Wright waited to convey him to Montreal. His family then accompanied the coffin to Quebec City where it lay in state in the Chateau of St Louis. On the fourth of September, 1819, his remains were finally interred in the Cathedral Church at Quebec after a large military funeral.

Meanwhile, on Chapman's Farm, beside the old road that still passes through Perth, there stands a simple cairn marking the spot where Richmond died. His life had come full circle—begun in a barn and ended in a barn. A rather ignoble end for one so nobly born.

The Red House, 55 Craig Street. Perth's oldest house, this oak log structure was built as Adamson's Inn in 1816, but it enjoyed wide usage as a church, school, meeting room, tavern and print shop in the settlement's early years. During his visit in 1819, the Duke of Richmond suggested painting the outside red. In 1822, the Red House was painted white and has remained misnamed ever since.
Credit: Perth Museum

Charles Lennox, 4th Duke of Richmond (1764-1819). After an undistinguished career in the British Army, Charles Lennox became a Member of Parliament (1790-1806) before inheriting the dukedom. From 1807-13, he served as Lord Lieutenant of Ireland and then went to Belgium where he participated in the Inniskilling Dragoons' desperate charge up Wavre Road during the Battle of Waterloo. In July 1818, he arrived in Quebec as Governor-in-Chief of the Canadas.
Credit: Public Archives of Canada.

View by J.P. Cockburn of Rideau portage, c. 1830.
Credit: Royal Ontario Museum.

PLAYFAIR'S PROGRESS

Mrs Playfair, the former Miss Sophia Cherry, was a pretty, silly, frivolous thing. She thrived on the social status she held as wife to a major in the Lanark militia and was known for her extravagant entertainments at which she served all sorts of expensive delicacies. She liked to pay calls, gossip, shop and leave the mundane responsibilities of running a household and raising her children to hired help. As servants were both expensive and difficult to keep in the egalitarian world of Upper Canada, affairs at home did not always run as smoothly as they should.

Nothing but the finest would do for Mrs Playfair. However, until the Tay and Rideau Canals were built by the early 1830s, all goods had to be brought overland to Perth by a rough trail cut through the bush from Brockville. So, even the purchase of everyday supplies was a financial strain, even on the half-pay pension of a militia major. This did not deter Mrs Playfair.

Everyone recognized Mrs Playfair while on her afternoon rounds. She always dressed in silk and sported a very pretty green parasol, so fashionable at the time. She looked more suited to the salons of Edinburgh than a backwoods village in Upper Canada.

Major Andrew Playfair was one of the dozens of half-pay officers who had taken advantage of the government's generous land grant offer to settle in the Perth Military Settlement following the War of 1812-14. Born in Paris in 1790, he was the son of William Playfair, author of *The History of Jacobism, France As It Is, Decline and Fall of Nations* and numerous other worthy works. He was educated in Edinburgh under the aegis of his uncle, a professor of natural history at Edinburgh University, and, at age sixteen, entered the British Army as an ensign in the 32nd Regiment to fight Napoleon. Playfair possessed an agile mind; in 1810, he was made second lieutenant in reward for designing a firearm highly valued by the Duke of York. A year later, he was promoted to first lieutenant in the 104th Regiment and sent to Ireland.

By 1813, the 104th Regiment had been transferred to Canada to fight the Americans. Here, Playfair distinguished himself at both Sackett's Harbour and on the Niagara Frontier, both brutal campaigns where every third man was killed or wounded.

Following peace, Lieutenant Playfair took advantage of the British government's generous offer to remain in Canada. As a lieutenant, he was entitled to 600 acres, a lot in town and a half-pay pension. He also achieved improved social standing by becoming a major in the Lanark militia. Rank was everything—even to a now significant landowner in the townships of Bathurst, Drummond and Lansdowne—in a community where one in five military settlers was an officer.

Major Playfair was imbued with the kind of enthusiasm that can only be found in a frontier settlement. Coming from an educated, if no longer moneyed, background (his family lost much after Andrew's birth in their escape from Paris during the French Revolution), his vision knew no bounds. In fact, he was determined to make his fortune and enhance his stature in this new land of opportunity. As owner of a large estate, he was confirmed with an undisputed respectability as well as the means to house, clothe and feed his family. Mother Earth would naturally give forth of her bounty and he would pursue the more intellectual pursuits of science. A perfect partnership. In this belief, he was a product of his age and class.

So to farming did he turn.

But first, he needed a big house. With great attention to detail, he laid out the plans for a stone manor which included a sweeping gravel drive up from the Mississippi River. He named it Renvie Lodge after the Playfairs' ancestral parish in Scotland.

Fortunately, he had invested in a boat-building enterprise, so he was able to economize on materials by purchasing in quantity. As long as his saw mill was producing boards for one endeavour, it might as well do the work for two.

Clearing his land of trees to make way for his home, and provide timber for his boats, inspired him to make more economies. The easiest way to remove tree stumps was to burn them off. Many settlers earned cash by carefully preserving the ashes of the burnt wood and selling them to potash manufacturers for, usually, sixpence a bushel—welcome money indeed. Potash was a valuable commodity, used for soap, and an important Canadian export. Sometimes, it was possible to pay for the clearing of the land with the potash.

Playfair, however, was not content to take his ashes to an established potashery. He elected instead to construct one of his own. This, he rationalized, would not only pay for the clearing of the land, but add another very profitable arm to his ever growing industrial empire. Industrialism was the hallmark of this turbulent post-war period, and he was determined to be a leader in the movement.

Potash is made by repeatedly pouring water over ashes. The water, which dissolves the alkali in the ashes, now contains lye and is allowed to drain out of holes punched through the bottom of the barrel to be caught in tubs. The lye of a barrel of ashes, boiled along with ten pounds of tallow, produces about forty pounds of very good, soft soap.

Potasheries were always built upon a running stream, the Mississippi being an ideal river for this purpose, Playfair rightly thought. However, he would need a pump to raise the water from the river and a platform with gutters to distribute the water to the many barrels, or leaches, containing the ashes. He would also need large boilers so as to reduce the lye to black salts. The black salts would then be heated to a high degree, 'til they were completely fused. By this process, all the impurities contained in the potash would be consumed and, upon cooling, it would be perfectly white and fit for market.

Riches from potash were as easy as falling off a log, he calculated.

Playfair set to work on his potash manufactory. He reassigned the men who had been working on his big house to the potashery. They protested somewhat as they had far from completed the house. Major Playfair would not hear any arguments on the advisability of finishing one project before beginning another, insisting that he would have even more money for the house once the potashery was operational.

Because of the new urgency to process the ashes, Major Playfair instructed his workers to transfer unused materials from the boat yard and house to the new site. Any arguments from the Reverend Bell, the family's minister, about robbing Peter to pay Paul, were shrugged off by the ever optimistic major. Work at both sites, however, soon ceased due to a lack of materials—and a shortage of cash.

An agile mind such as Major Playfair's is never idle for long. While Mrs Playfair continued to entertain society with luxuries many of her neighbours could only dream of, Major Playfair continued to be inspired by the possibilities of his new country. As he gazed over his land alongside the Mississippi, he gaped in awe with the expanse of it all. Centuries tall, the pine trees stood sentinel between past and future. It was up to him to breach their guard and seize their treasure. One by one, he attacked the trees and, one by one, he brought them down, their life-blood oozing into the ground at his feet. The battle sounds of industry waged around him while he walked through the carnage he had wrought. He looked down absently at his stained hands and tried to wipe the stickiness from his fingers. It was like tar. This was it! This was the gold that the trees had been guarding–pine tar.

And so to processing pine tar did Major Andrew Playfair turn.

Major Playfair was "neither lazy nor negligent," observed the Reverend Bell. "But, his brain was so fertile in new plans that he could never finish a tythe of them. He had so many irons in the fire that he burnt at least half of them."[1] He was also not helped in his schemes by his wife who, among many things, "knew but little of either the theory or practice of farming."[2]

[1] Rev. Wm. Bell Diaries, December 1824.
[2] Ibid.

As with his house, farm, boat works and potashery, Major Playfair never did complete the apparatus for making tar from pine tree roots. But, not to worry, when the major began to run into difficulties obtaining materials through local suppliers, he purchased his own waggon and horse team to drive goods from Brockville. Again, he saw this investment as both an economy and an asset to his over-extended industrial empire. Not only would he not have to pay cartage fees to someone else, but he could offset his costs by accepting commissions himself.

Well, this scheme would have worked if the horses had not died from over driving.

At about this time, a new opportunity presented itself that would allow both Major and Mrs Playfair to draw upon their respective strengths. They opened a store. Mrs Playfair certainly knew all there was to know about shopping for the very finest that money could buy and Major Playfair was unafraid of any venture about which he knew absolutely nothing.

Needless to say, the store did not succeed. Mrs Playfair was in charge, so no matter how much they sold, there just never seemed to be any money to pay the suppliers.

Undaunted by failure so far, Major Playfair returned to the source of his most inspired dreams—the Mississippi. In the early days of any settlement, the first industry to surface is milling. All that is needed to become a miller is to set up a water wheel and the appropriate apparatus at a set of rapids. An enterprising entrepreneur would begin by milling timber from the surrounding farms and then, as settlers planted and harvested crops, add grist and flour mills to his operation. The area surrounding the Perth Military Settlement was criss-crossed with streams and rivers jumbling over the thin, rocky soil, and throughout the region during the nineteenth century, a mill sprang up wherever water swiftly flowed.

Major Playfair was fortunate that his stretch of the Mississippi included a long run of rapids at the bottom of a long, straight stretch, creating both natural power and mill pond. The surrounding forests and burgeoning farms would provide him with an infinite supply of raw materials for an entire complex of mills—saw, grist and fulling. However, before Major Playfair could really commence on this latest venture, he was, unfortunately, imprisoned for debt.

During the major's imprisonment, Mrs Playfair and her children fell on hard times. By the time of his release, all of the Playfairs had been reduced to rags and bare feet. But, appearances had to be maintained. Although they could no longer afford a servant, Mrs Playfair continued to stay in bed 'til noon and refused, still, to do any household chores. The major tried his best, but Reverend Bell, on a pastoral call, remarked that the floor was, "like that of a ship's cabin after a storm . . . while the industrious husband with his shirt sleeves tucked up was baking bread upon a board to breakfast the hungry urchins around him."[3]

Major Playfair spent two years in prison. This was, as Reverend Bell so wryly put it, "a severe trial to his active and enterprising spirit."[4] He obtained the blessing of liberty after making appropriate arrangements with his creditors. One creditor opted to take possession of Playfair's still-uncompleted house and had it finished.

While incarcerated, the major had ample opportunity to reflect upon his miscalculations, but he remained committed to his industrial goals. After his release, he returned to his half-finished mills and set about making them operational. But Lady Luck continued to conspire against him. The mill dam, which is crucial for the control of water—and therefore power—to a mill, had been so improperly constructed that it did not retain any water at all. He did, however, have extremely fine burr stones for his grist mill, the first mill in the area to be so equipped.

It was while he pondered his next course of action that one of his creditors, who had not assented to the terms of his release, charged the constable to have him returned to prison. When the two appeared on his property (he did manage to regain his Mississippi home), Major Playfair fell back on his breeding, his status as a British subject and his training as an officer in His Majesty's Army, and stood up against the interlopers, armed with an axe. He defied his creditor and the constable to drag him, "to a dungeon like a felon."[5] The constable

[3] Ibid.
[4] Ibid.
[5] Ibid.

and the creditor prudently withdrew in search of reinforcements.

And so to the woods did Major Playfair retreat, until the insubordinate cur dropped all charges.

But nothing would keep Major Playfair down for long.

It was while a travelling Methodist preached in the area that Major Playfair next became inspired. The man's religious fervour so struck him, as the evangelist brought down the wrath of God from his pulpit on the stump, that he converted on the spot.

And so to preaching did Major Playfair turn.

He found his first converts amongst his family, and amongst some of his more wicked neighbours. Soon, however, he had gone beyond private conversations and was preaching publicly wherever he could find a lost soul to hear him. Despite his lack of training, and only rudimentary knowledge of the Bible, he never found himself at a loss for words and the presiding elder soon hired him to fill the place of second preacher on his local circuit. The forest was his temple and, as he had drawn inspiration from the trees for material gain, so did he now draw inspiration from them for spiritual growth. Since this was the style of the travelling Methodist preacher, it can be said that Major Playfair had finally found his true calling.

Despite the joy that Major Playfair felt from his new vocation, all was not bliss. He suffered difficulties in attracting a congregation. His many business failures did not encourage his neighbours to believe that he could manage their spiritual affairs with any guarantee of even purgatory, let alone heaven. But local laughter failed to daunt Major Playfair. Each Sunday, he would set off in his canoe up the Mississippi and gather a number of people to bring home and hear the Word.

Not to despair, 'though. His circuit riding gave him ample opportunity to explore the back country of Bathurst Township with a view to opening it up for further settlement. As a small village, appropriately named Playfairville, grew up around his mills, he became a vocal advocate of the necessity of colonization roads.

In 1837, the sabres of war rattled again. Uprisings in Upper and Lower Canada gave way to fear of invasion from the United States. And so did Major Playfair return to his first profession—soldiering.

As a loyal member of Her Majesty's Militia, Major Playfair saw it as his duty to volunteer as a field officer at the front. Unfortunately, however, the rebellions were quashed before he could mobilize his company, but he was still promoted to lieutenant-colonel of the Lanark Rifles for his gallant display of loyalty.

Things were definitely improving for Colonel Playfair.

As already mentioned, Colonel Playfair came from a family of letters and he carried on the family tradition with the same enthusiasm he brought to every endeavour. He frequently expressed himself on public and political issues through letters to local newspapers and in several pamphlets, including *Remarks on Mr. Justice Brown's Report to the committee appointed to promote the St. Lawrence and Lake Huron Railroad* (Perth, British Standard Office, 1852, 30pp) and *A Letter from a Volunteer of 1806 to the Volunteers of 1860* (Montreal, Lovell, 1860, 30pp). An excerpt of the latter follows:

> Although I have had the honour to hold Commissions in two Regiments of the line, viz. the 32nd and the 104th, yet in taking a retrospective view of my life, the day in which I exult the most is when as a stripling I stretched up to be taken into the ranks as a Volunteer in Old England, in 1806. Time cannot change the fixed principle within; the selfsame spirit swells my breast, the same heart beats for Britain's glory, the same hand that carried a sword in her defence now directs the pen, with no other view than rendering my humble assistance in the laudable volunteer movement, in defence of the nation . . .[6]

With eloquence such as this, it was only natural that Colonel Playfair would eventually turn to politics.

In 1857, Colonel Playfair stood for election as an independent in the riding of South Lanark in the Legislature for Canada West. For once, Colonel Playfair met with unqualified success as he handily defeated both his opponents:

[6] Jack Brown, <u>Olden Days in Playfairville,</u> Mallorytown, 1972.

Three cheers for Colonel Playfair!
What further need we say,
Than hope he'll vote as conscience bids
And give us all Fair play.[7]

Colonel Playfair did not waste this opportunity; he expounded upon all issues put before the Legislature. He advocated settlement of the west, lest the Americans move in with their republican ideals, as well as abolition of the Hudson's Bay Company's claims to this same region. He endorsed Queen Victoria's choice of Ottawa as the new capital of the country.

A man both ahead of and typical of his time, he outlined a plan for a combined water and rail route from the Atlantic to the Pacific (which eventually did come to pass) and agitated for a colonization road from Perth north-west to Buckshot Lake of which he, naturally, would serve as superintendent. Thwarted in this latter desire, one day Colonel Playfair set off to see John A. Macdonald who, he was sure, would immediately put matters to right.

After much shuffling about the corridors of power, the good colonel eventually tracked down John A. in a council meeting and demanded that he receive an audience, at once.

"God bless my soul, Colonel Playfair," exclaimed the minister, grasping him with both hands. "How are you? I'm so glad to see you. Bye-the-bye, Colonel, we have just been discussing in council a military matter that we cannot decide. Now you, with your great military experience and your memories of Salamanca and Talavera, will be able to solve the question."

The colonel drew himself up and looked grave.

"The question is," said John A., "how many pounds of powder put under a bull's tail would blow his horns off?"

And with that, the future Father of Confederation escaped back into his office leaving the good colonel feeling decidedly tweaked.[8]

But the trip had not been in vain. Upon his return home, he opened the mail bag (he also held the office of mail carrier between Perth and Playfairville) and discovered an official letter addressed to himself. It contained notice of his desired appointment.

45

---

[7] *Carleton Place Herald*, December 1857.
[8] Biggar, E.B. Anecdotal Life of Sir John A. Macdonald.
   Montreal: John Levell & Son, 1891. pp 198-200.

However, like many a politician before and since, Colonel Playfair got trapped between his own avowed beliefs and the temptations of the big city. He danced on a Sunday.

He claimed that while out walking one Sunday evening, he had merely dropped in to a social gathering given by Attorney-General Cartier at his home in St George's Square, Toronto. Reports that he had been "(tripping) the light fantastic toe,"[9] raised sufficient concern amongst the Methodist Conference that they intended to have the matter investigated. And, to rub salt in Colonel Playfair's already lacerated dignity, the Grumbler immortalized the event which the *Perth Courier* reprinted for all to judge:

Ye Gallant Colonel Playfair goeth to Ye Ball

Tell it not in Perth, let not the sound
thereof reach Lanark

Scene—Ye Big House of ye little Attorney General Cartier in St. George's Square.
Time—Half-past eight o'clock Sunday Evening, February 27th.

YE GALLANT AND REVEREND COLONEL
IS ANNOUNCED.

Cartier—(Going forward to meet him.)
  Ah! mon cher Colonel, how you do, old boy?
  I welcome you with veri mooch big joy:
  You are one jolly trump—by gar! me say
  We'll make ze hours fly vari quick away.
  I introduce you, and I tell you, sare,
  Ye shall forget you have ze milk-white hair;
  You leetle rogue, me find you one maimselle
  To be your partner in ze next quadrille.
  Ah! ah! me make one joke—sare, while you stay,
  You, Meester Playfair, give your heels fair play;
  Me warn you though—beware ze Cupid's dart
  Don't make ze leetle hole, sare, in your heart.

Playfair—(Who appears nervous and uneasy.)
  Hush, brother Cartier—hem, excuse me, Sir,
  Mr., I mean—I really must defer,
  Today less sacred, such unhallowed fun;
  How to lost sinners shall I dare to preach,

[9] *Perth Courier*, 18 March 1859.

Poor, ruined souls of Lanark, if this breech
Of Heaven's command I boldly perpetrate?
No, Sir! we ministers must at any rate,
For fear this wicked world should sneer and snuffle,
Daren't try on Sabbath day the "Double Shuffle."

Cartier– Ha! ha! he! one very pretty joke
Ze double shuffle—why you then have poke
One leetle fun at me—now come, by gar! mon cher,
You shall not be one reverend ministaire,
You are, ze Colonel Playfair, who have been
One gallant soldier of our gracious queen;
Ze priest may pray, ze soldier sare should feast;
I have invite ze soldier, not ze priest,
Diable, mon cher, you shall be ruled by me,
And have one vat you call it? leetle spree.

Playfair– My Christian brother (aside—may the fates go hang,
I can't forget my usual Sunday twang.)
My dear—ahem!—confound, Cartier, you
Have no conception what a storm would brew
Among the Lanark boobies, if they knew
I showed my sanctimonious phiz at all
Within a furlong of a Sunday ball.
The very thought of that prospective shrine
Makes me feel faint,—old fellow, where's the wine?
I think a glass or two would do me good.

Cartier– Ah! oui, you leetle rouge (sic), of course it would.
What you will have? Champagne—this way, old boy
By gar! mon cher, I make you dance for joy.
Ze leetle bubbles in ze wine, again
Shall frisk, and dance, sare, in your leetle brain.
It is tres bon, one—two—you take another,
Then you no call me more, ze Christian brother.

Playfair– Thankee, don't mind, by Jove, you are a trump;
Hang me, old fellow if I care a dump
What folks may say, guess now I'll take fill;
And if I like to dance, why dance I will.
Fill up, old boss—one more—come shine or rain,
And Lanark's Playfair is himself again.
Hence with all thoughts of sanctimonious snuffle,
I'm game, old fellow, for the double shuffle.

Cartier– Bravo! mon Colonel, I you love quite hot,

Now you have sent ze ministair to pot;
Now you have say ze leetle word "don't care,"
You are once, twice, three times more welcome, sare.
Ze blue-eyed and ze black-eyed jolie dame?
You no var mood partecklar—then me say,
You dance with both to give them fair play;
But Colonel, come, we'll have before we join
Ze jolies dames one leetle glass more wine?

Playfair– Perhaps you don't think, old boss, I'm up to snuff,
But sir, I kind o' guess I've had enough,
However, why, I calculate I'll take
Just one glass more—it can't much difference make.

Cartier– Ha, ha! me see the frisky leetle bubble
Make you feel good, but mind you no see double.
Saint mon Colonel, now you come with me,
I introduce you to ze fair lady.
(They go to join the ladies.)

Ye reverent Colonel is introduced to a charming little nymph with flowing ringlets, and grows gallant.

Playfair—(with a low bow and a benignant smirk.)
May I have the supreme felicity of dancing the next quadrille with Madamoiselle?

Nymph with the ringlets–
Avec grand plasir Monsieur.

Playfair—(Insinuating smile.)
Is Madamoiselle fond of dancing?

Nymph– Oh oui! et vous aussi Monsieur?

Playfair–I,—oh yes! extremely. Madamoiselle, especially with (low bow) so fair a partner.

Nymph–Monsieur est bien gallant.

The music strikes up and Playfair undauntedly faces it.

Oh! it is a glorious sight to witness the hoary-headed soldier treading the mazes of the dance. Advance—military erectness. Retire—exquisite grace. Turn partner—charming smile and the slightest possible (of course involuntary) pressure of the little hand that trembles in his. Set to partner—Bouxary thrown in the shade. Cross over—youthful agility and a faultless chassez. Bow—body bent, and a graceful wave of the hand, attended with tremendous effect. Finish—partner led off in triumph, and Playfair the acknowledged lion of the room.

(Cartier advances to congratulate him.)

Cartier–   Bravo! mon Colonel, I you vari much
Congratulate you have ze finish touch,
You are ze artiste sare in every part;
By gar! you rogue you turn ze ladies heart.
You have two, three, six, rare, conquests made,
And put ze gentilshomes all in ze shade.

Playfair–   Why yes, old boss, I guess now I can come
A kind of graceful double shuffle, some,
But I say, Cartier, do you—do you think
I really made six conquests?

Cartier–   Do me tink?
Of course me tink, me know you have you rogue,
You lucky dog, you will be all ze vogue.
Have me no heard ze lots of ladies say
They like to kiss ze dear old Colonel—eh?

Ye gallant Colonel is in extacies and begs to be introduced all round; in the meantime the curtain falls and leaves him "ze lion of ze Ball."

Scene 2nd—Time half-past one o'clock, a.m., Monday.

Ye gallant Colonel takes his leave. During his walk home his head is in a continuous whirl; fair faces are still flitting before him; bewitching eyes are gazing at him, charming smiles are still greeting him; but is he quite happy? Alas! no, an indistinct feeling that something is wrong troubles him. Ah! he has it at length; he remembers it was Sunday night; then he thinks of his Brother Ministers of his class meetings—of his constituents in Lanark, and devoutly hopes that neither they, nor the Globe will ever hear of his presence at ze Ball.[10]

Colonel Playfair did not serve a second term and to his home on the Mississippi did he retire.

After a long, stimulating and complex life, where every challenge was an incentive, Colonel Playfair died peacefully and quietly in his bed on the first day of September, 1868, in his seventy-ninth year.

---

[10] Ibid.

. . . He was a man of kind and generous disposition, gentlemanly and courteous to all, ready to give of his means, and to cheer and encourage the distressed; a warm friend, a fond parent, a kind husband, a sincere christian, and a loyal subject.

His health had been declining for some time past, but on the first of September he took a sudden attack of illness, and within an hour afterwards he departed this life, in perfect peace, without a lingering groan, and fully trusting in Him who is able to save.[11]

Colonel Andrew Playfair (1790-1868).
Courtesy of the Perth Museum.

[11] *Perth Courier*, 11 September 1868.

SAVE YOUR ASHES!!!
THE Subscriber will pay the highest
Price for
HOUSE ASHES.
GEORGE ELLIS.
Perth, 27th Oct. 1886.

Advertisements like this one in the *Bathurst Courier* were
very common. Ashes were used to make soap and any not
needed for household use were sold for much-welcomed
cash.

Poster showing the results of the 1857 election.
Credit: Perth Museum.

THE FERRYMAN'S WELCOME

The narrows that slashed the road between Brockville and Perth were treacherous, whether you travelled by water or land. A storm on the Rideau Lakes could whip the waves to heights that towered over a full-grown man. And to cross, you had to engage the services of John Oliver, ferryman.

Oliver was a necessary evil. His ferry wasn't much more than a raft of logs lashed together propelled with two oars, but it was the only way to get across. It forwarded staples, livestock and goods as well as pedlars, farmers, missionaries, immigrants, soldiers, trappers and itinerants from one side of the narrows to the other.

It was a good business, yet Oliver and his family displayed more wealth than was really possible for a backwoods ferryman to accumulate by honest means. And that was the rub; John Oliver was not an honest man.

In fact, John Oliver was a thoroughly villainous man. He and his son controlled this stretch of the Rideau, back in the days when the canal was still more fancy than fact, with a reign of terror not seen before or since. He exacted demanding tolls from travellers—three pence for foot passengers and fifteen pence for waggons—and menaced everyone within his reach. A blackened eye, a missing cow or a tumbled shed were all shrugged off as "accidents" by the locals. For it was eight, long miles to Perth and the authorities and, in these parts, John Oliver had more might than any drill sergeant on parade.

However, Oliver's Ferry aside, travelling between Brockville and Perth was hazardous at the best of times. The "road" was a broken track that wound its way through swamps and bush. It was not uncommon for a tree, blown down by a storm, to lie across the road for several months until it came time for statute labour when, once a year, landowners were required to volunteer their labours for local improvements. So, depending on the season . . . In the meantime, travellers were forced to make their own way around any obstacles.

Smart people travelled in groups, as it was very easy to get lost in the thick bush. However, occasionally, there would be a lone soul who just couldn't wait for a companion, and it was to these that John Oliver was his most solicitous.

William Grange thought that he would never be dry again. He had left Brockville early that morning on foot, and it was imperative that he reach Perth that day, a distance of some thirty miles. He had it on good authority that this was possible, but that was if you didn't get lost, which William Grange most assuredly was. Forward looked the same as backward, left the same as right. The greens and browns of the bush blurred before his eyes, the pattern so expertly and intricately woven that barely a scrap of blue peeked through. And nowhere in the suffocating bush was there anything resembling a trail. With each step, mud and ooze dragged at his boots and brambles clutched at his coat in a struggle that William felt he would surely lose. He should have hired a horse. That would have tripled his rate of speed to six miles an hour but, then again, he would still be lost on top of trying to keep the poor beast from being swallowed up by this godforsaken excuse for a road.

What was that ahead? William couldn't believe his eyes. It was an orchard, coming into bloom. That meant high ground—dry ground—and an opportunity to make up some time. He climbed the rise and walked into the centre of this unexpected Eden. He took a deep breath and closed his eyes. The soft scent from the blossoms cleared the miasmas from his head. The buzzing he heard was that of fat, lazy bumble-bees collecting sweet nectar, not the incessant drone of thousands of mosquitoes draining him dry of sense and life. Oh, he could die here and call it bliss!

A low bellow wakened him from his reverie. A snort, like a kettle blowing off its lid, turned him to face the largest, meanest-looking bull he'd ever met on the wrong side of a fence.

"Nice bossy," William cajoled as he edged backwards, "nice bossy." The bull, disagreeing, shook his head, pawed the ground and snorted again. Through the trees, William could see several cows coming up behind the bull to see what all the fuss was about. The bull hunched its massive shoulders. "Oh, Lord," moaned William beneath his breath. "Just what I need. A bull intent on proving himself before the ladies."

"Alright, Sir Bossy. I bow before your superior manhood. Now, if you will just allow me a graceful retreat . . ." The bull had been stalking back and forth in the front of his herd, giving them plenty of opportunity to compare his virility against that of the cringing man before them. The cows, discovering that plenty of sweet grass grew in the orchard, murmured amongst themselves and paid little attention to the show.

William, meanwhile, was paying little attention to where his feet were taking him. Keeping a sharp eye on the affronted bull, he had been gradually edging his way backwards. As the distance between them lengthened, William started to relax. A few more steps and he would be . . . Rocks and thorns clawed at his face and pricked through his coat as he tumbled down the side of the steep hill, then—SPLAT!

"Christ! Another mud-hole."

William tried to extricate himself from the mud's clinging fingers, but it took several attempts before he could shake them off and reach firmer land. Ahead, he could see that some small trees had been felled to form a crude bridge over the muck. "At least," he grunted to himself, "I've fallen down the side with the road." Balancing himself with a staff made from a small sapling, William continued his way north and west, only occasionally slipping back into the swamp.

The sun was grinning from high in the sky when William finally caught a glimpse of broad water through the trees. His unexpected mud bath had provided some protection from the mosquitoes, but the odour nearly overwhelmed him. He gratefully let the sweet lake breezes fill his lungs. He plunged his arms and face into the water and let cool rivulets stream down his neck. A minute later, he had stripped off his soiled garments and surrendered himself to the soft caresses of the Rideau. Spent, he dragged himself up on the shore and collapsed on the soft grass. Within minutes, the sun had soothed away the worries of the day, and he was asleep.

William felt delicate fingers tickle his ears—the lightest of touches that sent cool shivers down his spine. He stretched contentedly, rolled over and exposed his near naked body to the full embrace of his temptress, but her mood abruptly changed from coy and teasing to cold and scornful. She slapped an icy hand across his face, blinding him temporarily as he vainly reached out to hold her to him. But, like quicksilver, she slipped through his fingers and left him shivering. Her jeers soon turned to shrieks as he lay huddled on the ground until he suddenly realized that it wasn't a woman who scorned him, but the wind. As he cleared the water from his eyes, he realized that the weather had changed while he had slept by the lake. The welcoming sun of earlier in the day was snuggling down below the horizon, drawing a thick coverlet of clouds over its head. It was a stiff breeze that had stirred the waves into rousing him from his tryst with the capricious nymph. He looked around him in panic. Any adversities that William had faced already that day were mere inconveniences compared to the possibility of spending a night in the bush. Although he imagined their greedy eyes and hungry teeth with every rustle in the grass, wolves, bears and wild cats almost paled in ferocity when he allowed himself to think—even briefly—of the kelpies, goblins or other wee folk that might inhabit this uncivilized land.

Fragments of conversation blown apart by the wind grabbed William's attention. Two men, barely visible in the gathering gloom, were talking as they lashed down a large barge. The ferry! William scrabbled to his feet, madly retrieving his scattered clothes, and sped towards the quay.

"Wait! I want to go across."

William's words were snatched away by the rising wind, and the two men continued with their chores.

"Wait!"

The elder of the two stopped and turned as William stumbled and fell, almost at their feet. William looked up and gasped as flickering tongues of flame wreathed a blackness that seemed to suck out his very soul. Paralysing fear gripped his defenceless body as he cowered, blinded, before this sinister force. A gnarled limb reached towards him and the blackness swirled grotesquely in its molten halo. William ceased to breathe, ceased to think, ceased to act. Instead, he felt himself drawn towards this manifestation of Satan.

"Watch y'self."

William blinked at the harsh face before him—it was human!—which he could now clearly see by the red glow that barely clung to the horizon.

"Oh," he gasped, leaning backwards. "I'm looking for the ferryman." William's knees were trembling, whether from fear or fatigue, he could not tell.

"I'm the ferryman," grunted the man—he was a man, wasn't he? He was still badly shaken by the illusion he had seen. "John Oliver. M' son, William." A younger version of the ferryman turned towards William.

"Oh, that's my name too."

`What an idiotic thing to say,' thought William hysterically. `I've got to pull myself together. This man is not the devil. My mind's just playing tricks on me in the dark. And who could blame it after the day I've had.'

"Then I would like to book passage to cross immediately, ferryman," he stated, vainly attempting to instill some authority in his voice. "It's imperative that I reach Perth as soon as possible."

"Can't be done," replied John Oliver, as he turned to help his son.

"No, you don't understand," whined William, becoming pathetic. "I can pay." William reached into his coat for his purse. Despite its current condition, you could still tell that the garment was of fine material and had been tailored by an expert hand. His trousers had been new, and his boots, although sadly dulled by the day's abuses, were obviously fashioned of good leather especially for him.

John Oliver had paused briefly at William's interruption. Flicking a glance over the bedraggled man, he repeated, "Can't be done," and proceeded up from the shore with his son.

"I thought you were the ferryman, Mister Oliver," William asserted sharply, in a bid to convey confidence and submerge his rising anxiety. "I can't really speak for this god-forsaken corner, but, in most places of the world, that means you transport people across water for money. I wish to go across, I have money and you are the ferryman. So, step to it!"

By the end of this little speech, William was feeling more like the successful gentleman he really was. He had drawn himself up to his full height and projected the air of one who was used to having his orders obeyed, immediately.

"Can't go across."

"My good man," William blew his calm air with a gust of exasperation.

"The wind's up and the sun's down. Can't go across."

William suddenly realized that it was now quite dark. Thick clouds rolled relentlessly across the sky, stomping out the full moon, and crested waves threw themselves angrily against the shore. He shivered.

`What am I to do?' he thought dismally.

"Come up t' th' hoose an' th' wife'll fix ye up fer the night. She always has a mess o' stew on the go."

William's head jerked up. Could the man read his thoughts? There was something very eerie about him. William continued to stand frozen by the lake shore, unsure what to do. It was the rain that finally prompted him to follow John Oliver into the dark.

The rain was coming down in sheets when William was finally welcomed into the comforting glow of Mrs Oliver's kitchen. His ruined coat steamed before the fire, and a thick bowl of tasty stew spread warmth through his body. John and

William Oliver ate their suppers silently while Mrs Oliver prattled about, obviously pleased with the unexpected company.

"Oh, Mister Grange, ye kinna know what a delight it is to have you grace our humble home this even'. Noo, of course, 'tis a shame that you kinna make Perth afore th' morrow, but my mon will na cross th' Rideau once the sun goes doon. I'm sure your people will understand—the dangers of travelling at dark, ye ken. Plus, she's a ticklish mistress, th' Rideau, an' it dinna do no good to cross her when she gets uppity, like t'night." Mrs Oliver laughed at her own joke as she continued with her evening bustling.

William looked around the single room and wondered where he would spend the night. Although he was grateful to the Olivers for their Christian charity, he did not feel completely at ease sleeping under the same roof as them. Mrs Oliver's non-stop chatter explained John and William Oliver's taciturnity—did William speak at all?—but there was just something about them. Even Mrs Oliver, a pleasantly plump widgeon, had an air about her that William could just not put his finger on.

"Noo, Mister Grange . . ."

"About the fare for board and lodging . . ."

"Och, Mister Grange. Dinna fret aboot that t'night. You kin settle up wit' m'mon on the morrow, when you goes on your way. But, afore then, you needs a place to bed doon. There's some nice clean straw in the byre. You jist grab a lantern there and William will take ye oot."

William Oliver was standing by the open door and took the lantern from William before leading him out into the storm. It was pitch black, and the driving rain stung William's eyes shut. He couldn't see how the lantern could shed any light on their route, but, somehow, the ferryman's son led him through the inky darkness and William suddenly found himself out of the rain and inside the barn. The smell of damp hay filled his nostrils and the sound of rain drumming on the roof drowned his ears. However, as he stood there, trying to wipe the blindness from his eyes, he realized that he wasn't alone. "William?" He took a tentative step forward.

"Aaaargh!"

A whip-like thing snapped across his chest and tore at his head. Arms flailing, William turned to escape but didn't take two steps before he was knocked flat on his back. Raging fear propelled him backwards across the floor away, he hoped, from these familiars of Satan. The wall of the barn stopped him cold and he clawed at the logs in a futile attempt to force an opening. The demons started to wail their death chant and the barn shook from their lust. He could feel their breath on his neck and he knew that he had met his end.

"Mooo."

It was a cow! It was a god-damned cow. 'Of course it's a cow', thought William giddily, 'this is a barn. What else would be in a barn besides a cow?'

"Meow."

A soft, furry cat jumped on his lap and started picking at his clothes. That's what had clawed at his head. It must have jumped from the rafters. William's hand dropped to the cat's head and he started scratching its ears, so relieved that the demons were, again, only imaginary. 'This night will be the death of me if I don't calm down', thought William as he gathered straw for his bed. Thinking that ferrymen are devils and cows are demons. Hah!

So, with a smile on his face and the cat curled up at his waist, William soon fell asleep.

It had stopped raining. But that wasn't what had wakened William. In fact, there was no sound at all in the pre-dawn darkness. William stayed perfectly still, every nerve stretched out to find whatever it was that was waiting for him in the barn. He could sense that this being wanted him.

All the previous day's fears came rushing over William in a cold sweat, freezing him into immobility. Out of the darkness, hands seized his throat, gorging his tongue until it filled his mouth. His eyes strained at their sockets, desperate to see who his murderer was, and his ears throbbed with Death's screams.

Finally, the body stopped twitching. The hands that had been frantically picking at Death's vice grip fluttered into the straw and lay still. The door opened. A rising breeze swirled into the barn and then flew out, heavenward, only to be trapped by the trees standing guard around the killing ground.

The sun cautiously peeped its head above the horizon, and the songbirds fluttered at a new day washed clean by the storm. Mrs Oliver chatted away to no one in particular as she prepared breakfast. William came out of the barn carrying a shovel and nodded to his father. John acknowledged his silent message, then turned away and headed down to the quay where a group of travellers waited to cross, idly flipping a gold coin as he went.

Epilogue

John Oliver and his son William operated the ferry at Oliver's Landing—now known as Rideau Ferry—from 1816 until 1832. Years after they had ceased to terrorize the countryside, a shack that stood on their lot on the south shore of the Rideau, beside the present day bridge, was razed. Found beneath were human skeletons buried together in a massive grave. Since there had never been an epidemic of this proportion in the area, who could they have been? Perhaps those who had found a welcome with the ferryman.

Sepia and pencil drawing of Oliver's Ferry by J.P. Cockburn, 20 August 1830. John Oliver arrived in Perth in 1816 as part of the assisted emigrant scheme from Scotland. He quickly established a ferry on the south bank of the Rideau, as the military had reserved the more logical north bank, although he did not receive a licence to do so until 1820. Oliver was universally loathed, yet his licence did state that he was "a fit and proper person to have a licence for a Ferry."
Credit: Public Archives of Canada.

THE DEVIL AND
THOMAS EASBY

Thomas Easby had one goal in life—to be full. He didn't just want to be drowsily full, nor did he want to be button-busting full. He wanted to be so full that his eyes would squeeze shut in ecstasy over his expanding bulk. His fingers would rival in size the most succulent sausages, and his thighs would challenge a smoke house full of heroic hams. Oh, the imagined bliss of it all. And he would achieve this state not just on oatcakes and ale, but on dates stuffed with marzipan, potted salmon, black buns and thick, rich custards made with dozens of eggs—all washed down with gallons and gallons of hot, steaming atholl brose topped with whipped cream and toasted oatmeal. Mmmmmmm.

There was certainly no room for this dream in the farms and tenements of the Old Country, where each crumb was prized amongst a populace spent by war and starved by over-crowding. But in Upper Canada? There a man could lay claim to any dream he desired on a quarter section of virgin wilderness. It was his for the asking. However, it wasn't until Thomas Easby had walked his family the five miles north of the Perth Military Settlement to their new home in Drummond Township that he began to doubt his dream. On either side of the rough road were dense forests of pine, maple, cedar and oak that denied any hint of Ol' Sol until he was well up in the sky. Those who had come before him had managed to carve out pocket-sized farms, but the thick stumps studding the fields testified more strongly than the Reverend William Bell's *Hints to Emigrants* of the back-breaking labour facing every settler who wanted to own his future.

Thomas Easby began questioning his sanity in abandoning the devil he knew for this strange, unfamiliar world.

Rough paths that even oxen had difficulty travelling over were all that linked him to remote neighbours and villages. Mosquitoes, mud and long days of never-ending chores tormented him in summer, while waist-high snows, biting frosts and storms that smothered all human contact for days and weeks on end numbed him in winter. Yet, like many others, he continued to believe that he was better off as a landholder in the harsh wilderness of Upper Canada than as a crofter in Scotland.

All those who knew Thomas Easby saw a sober, hard-working, quiet family man. So, when the Easby home in Drummond Township burned to the ground on a cold December night in 1828, killing Mrs Easby and four of her children, most concentrated on consoling the shocked widower and his only surviving son.

When the ashes had cooled, the neighbours set about retrieving what remained of the bodies for a proper Christian burial. The children, still lying peacefully in their beds, were badly burned, and the wife, easily identified by her pregnant form, had obviously suffered a severe wound on her head during the tragedy. She and her children were solemnly laid to rest.

The surviving boy, four-year-old Joseph, was fostered out to neighbours, the Richardsons, while his father, Thomas, set about rebuilding a life for them.

Joseph kept pretty much to himself and wouldn't play with the Richardson children. Mrs Richardson left the boy alone to deal with his grief in his own way but kept a sharp eye on him so that she could comfort him when the time came.

After a few days, she noticed that young Joseph played the same game over and over again. As he recited the names of his siblings, he would whack a stick against the ground and laugh. This game continued every day for several weeks.

When she asked the boy if she could play the game too, he said it was his father's game and only he could play it.

Concerned, Mrs Richardson related the boy's strange behaviour to John Balderson, a member of the inquest which had been held at the time of the fire. All at the inquest had believed Easby's version of an accident. He was, as everyone knew, an honest, law-abiding family man.

The Perth authorities were informed, and a second inquest was called for early in February 1829. However, before this inquest could begin, Easby admitted his crime to John Balderson and James Young, the Perth gaoler, and was arrested on February second.

Easby was by far the most notorious inmate who had ever been held in the Perth gaol. Most miscreants were imprisoned for relatively minor offences, and at this time, the only other inhabitants were five debtors and a very penitent housebreaker named Molesworth. Easby seemed to quite enjoy his new surroundings and became a model prisoner.

One day in August 1829, the Reverend William Bell paid a pastoral call on the accused murderer. Mr Young, the gaoler, ushered in the Presbyterian minister with the curt warning, "Ye still won't get much out o' 'im."

Bell did not pay much attention to the gaoler's words, his attention focused entirely on the sinner before him. What he saw was the same as he had seen on every other visit he had made to Thomas Easby: a man at peace with himself. Bell continued with his now established ritual of divine service and admonitions to repent. Easby also maintained the pattern that he had established on previous visits. He acknowledged Bell's presence with a polite greeting but made no other effort either to reject or welcome the minister's words.

Bell sighed silently to himself as he made ready to leave. Just as he raised his fist to the door to summon Mr Young, Easby spoke,

"I was raised in the Church of England."

Bell turned.

"I would like to die that way."

Easby turned his back on Bell and looked out the window to the walled yard of the gaol. Bell was startled at this unexpected reference to any possible outcome of the trial which was to begin on Monday, August seventeenth. In fact, if anything, Easby had become even more uninterested in pleas, threats and cajoling to make peace with God and his fellow man as the trial date crept closer. He offered no insight into the reasons for his crimes and, after his initial confession, replied with indifference to any questions as to why he had murdered his family. The only topic that Easby found interesting was food.

Easby had an excellent appetite. Supplies from his farm were brought in at regular intervals, and he savoured the plain but hearty dishes made from his own flour, pork, butter and other foodstuffs. He became quite fat.

It was hard to imagine that such a quiet, almost gentle man could have committed such a crime. Was this the same man his four dead children and pregnant wife had known? The man of God could not penetrate his shield, but had the Devil?

For the Devil is a tempting fellow . . . charming and ever so willing to accommodate a man's every desire . . . for a price, of course. And what was Easby's desire? Why food, of course.

The Devil had lots of food. Food that Easby had been unable to provide for his family. The rocky, stump-strewn soil of Drummond Township had reluctantly given up only a few bushels of wheat and potatoes that fall, and it was not nearly enough to feed his five young children. And there would be a sixth before spring.

Then one day, as Easby sat down for his meal, the Devil thrust his failure in his face. The bairns, dressed in tattered and patched clothing, were inhaling their bowls of thin gruel and dry bread when the Devil asked him in a whiny voice, "How can they eat it so quickly when it took you so long, and so much work, to grow? Where is their gratitude?" he snivelled. "Why aren't they in awe of the miracle you have wrought?" Easby sputtered, his gruel dribbling down his chin. Suddenly, the Devil spat, "They are just like savages. They have no respect, nor do they value your power to create this most precious thing—food." Easby dropped his spoon, shaken by the Devil's fury. "In fact," the Devil stomped, "they don't deserve it!" And the force of his cloven hoof rattled the empty bowls.

Easby looked up to see his wife, Ann, glance at him, slight irritation crossing her worn face. "Thomas," she observed, "you are shaking the table." Easby looked down and saw hands—familiar, yet foreign—gripping the rough boards like vices. Ann gave a small gasp and passed her hand gently over her distended belly while she tried to settle herself more comfortably. The rage coursed up Easby's arms and seized his mind. That unborn child was sucking the life out of his house! he suddenly realized. He watched his wife cut her boiled potatoes into tiny bites, to make them last longer, but the unborn bairn greedily devoured every last one of them before they could reach her stomach. It thrived as his wife wasted. Easby understood that now.

He watched Ann carefully as she undressed that night. Yes! The babe in its soft, warm womb was looking over its plump shoulder and laughing at him. Laughing because it was growing fat and everyone else was growing thin.

"What will happen when the demon babe finally snaps the cord that binds it to its lair?" The Devil tormented his mind, demanding answers for questions Easby didn't want to ask. "Will it steal food from you, then? Will it eat every potato, every sausage, every last grain of wheat, all the while growing bigger and bigger and fatter and fatter until it bursts the walls of this house like it will burst the walls of your wife's body?"

Easby shook his head in denial at the Devil's taunts and his body trembled in disbelief as the Devil laughed his scorn.

"Are you cold, Thomas?" asked his wife. "Come closer to the fire, then, and I'll put another log on."

Easby looked at the flames and saw the Devil dancing from one log to the next. The Devil snapped and cackled with glee and then leapt up the chimney in a puff of smoke. Once outside, the Devil raced 'round and 'round the tiny shanty, the deep December snow swirling in his wake, and then darted in at one crack and then another to tease Easby with his long, icy fingers—behind the ears, the back of the neck—and then the Devil embraced Easby with such force that the whole shanty shook.

"Quite a storm we're in for tonight," commented Ann as she straightened the room in preparation for bed. The children slept peacefully on their straw pallets in the far corner of the one-room shanty. The only light came from the fire on the open hearth, and his wife's innocent movements cast grotesque shadows, which danced fiendishly against the walls. Her misshapen body took on fantastic forms as she moved around the room. First tall and spindly as a hemlock, her scrawny arms bent awkwardly, and then round and squat as a porcupine. But not once did her belly go through any metamorphosis. In fact, for a brief instant, it was all that was reflected upon the rough-hewn walls. Suspended in space, it had swallowed his wife.

"That's what bairns do, Easby," whispered the Devil, his pointed ear cocked to the sighs of the children's steady breathing. "They eat all that they touch. Aye, and if you don't act soon, there'll nay be a crumb left to nibble. E'en a mouse will turn his back on this barren hovel."

A child in the corner quietly whimpered.

"What is it, my love?" asked her mother.

"I'm hungry, ma."

"We all be hungry, dear. Try to sleep."

The Devil shrieked with maniacal glee outside the hut. Suddenly, he flew like the wind across the roof, down the smoke hole and knocked the logs across the open hearth. Sparks shot from his heels as he skidded to a halt right in front of Easby.

"No!" roared Easby.

"Yes," hissed the Devil.

"No," wailed Easby as he grabbed a blazing beech stick from the hearth and swung it at the Devil, scattering burning logs across the room.

At once, pandemonium seized the tiny hut. Easby, a man possessed, tore around the single room swinging at everything and everyone. Flames from the broken fire licked at the walls and, liking what they tasted, began to eat the dry wood with a voracious appetite.

One by one, Easby silenced the screams. At each child, he raised the stick with both hands, high above his head, and brought it crashing down on the small body. It was just like threshing wheat. Once, twice, thrice . . . with each swing, Easby heard the Devil shout out in encouragement the name of the now dead child. However, as he raised his arms for the fifth time, the boy laughed, and he was stopped by the most unearthly sound. It was as if all the lost souls of eternity had descended to this tiny corner of burning hell. And they had found an outlet for their pain in the voice of Easby's wife.

Easby turned and looked straight into the eyes of Death. The banshee—her eyes glazed, her long hair streaming and her ragged clothes tipped with fire—screamed through the burning air, her claws reaching out for his neck. For an instant, Easby stood frozen, unable to move or cry out. Then he saw the demon babe, trying vainly to hide itself in the folds of the banshee's skirts, and he swung.

Down came the burning roof and up leapt the Devil, turning back flips across the crusted fields. He left blackened footprints that melted the snow as he fled into darkness. Only a small boy remained to mourn the loss of a dream as he huddled in fear behind the byre.

On Friday, August twenty-first, 1829, the jury quickly rejected Easby's plea of "not guilty" and Judge Sherwood of the Court of King's Bench condemned him to hang by the neck until dead.

Although no previous announcement had been made for the time of the execution, crowds began pouring into Perth from all quarters soon after daylight, Monday the twenty-fourth. This was an event not to be missed. It was the first time there had ever been an execution in Perth, and everyone who was anyone—and especially those who weren't—was there.

A carnival atmosphere soon wended its way through the throngs filling the streets around the brick courthouse and gaol. Hucksters, buskers and preachers hawked their wares to anyone who would stand and listen. Mr Adams, a Methodist preacher, strategically positioned his father's waggon near the courthouse and used it as a platform from which to preach a very intensive, although irregular, sermon. Kegs of ale were brought forth, and many slaked their thirst as the hot August sun slowly marched overhead. Noon struck.

Thomas Easby was brought forth, bound and guarded by his gaolers. With steady steps they mounted the platform that had been constructed on the courthouse lawn. Great cries of derision rose up from the crowd to greet the condemned man, and many remarked in astonishment to their neighbours how fat Thomas Easby had become. Would the gibbet hold him? they mocked, or would it snap before the rope could snap his neck?

"Does the condemned man have any parting words?"

"Justice has been done," he replied.

The hangman placed the hood over Thomas Easby's head and adjusted the halter around his fat neck while the assembled hurled insults. The Reverend Michael Harris of the Church of England opened his Bible and began reading in an audible and pathetic tone. "Forgive us our trespasses as we forgive . . ."

The executioner let fall the trap-door.

An hour later, they cut Easby's body down. After a brief interment in the Church of England cemetery, the body was exhumed and handed over to Dr Wilson and two of his medical students for dissection. Their laboratory, in an old shanty about a mile away, became a popular site, and returning visitors soon told tales of the medical men converting the body into medicine for the use of the sick. Castor oil was being made from his fat and quinine from his brains, they said, and those with money to spare could purchase small squares of Easby's tanned hide—prices went as high as two dollars!—which made very durable wallets.

Such was the horror these tales caused that the families who lodged Dr Wilson and his students prohibited them from dining at the same table as they. And such was the end of a man who wanted nothing more than to eat his fill—and killed to do it.

Detail of watercolour by J.P. Cockburn (c. 1830) showing the formidable forests that faced the early settlers who came to the Perth Military Settlement.
Credit: Public Archives of Canada.

A native of Douglas, Lanarkshire, Dr James Wilson graduated from the University of Edinburgh in 1818 and emigrated to Perth in 1821, where he built a large and lucrative practice. The first civilian surgeon/ physician of note in the District of Bathurst, the "wee doctor" was described as an attentive and skilful physician who was known for his sense of humour. A respected amateur geologist, he discovered the feldspars, Wilsonite and Perthite, before returning in 1869 to Edinburgh, where he died in 1881.
Credit: Perth Museum.

THE BOYS OF THE BACKROOM

"I am ashamed," he thundered, his voice vibrating with displeasure. "Ne'er before has there been such a community in all of Christendom so lacking in public spirit."

The congregated jerked as one before Morris' verbal volley, and the flickering lamps trembled as Perth's most powerful man challenged the room. His strong arms flung shadows behind him where they scrabbled like sycophants, tumbling and colliding with each other in the wake of his frenzy. Small puffs of vapour punctuated Morris' denunciation of his neighbours, temporarily obscuring him from view. Grasping the courtroom rail, he punched his face through the cloud of frozen mist and glared. His head, wreathed in white, appeared to hover; his eyes, steely blue, mesmerized all who gazed into their depths.

For this was a matter of vital importance to the community. Its very tomorrow depended upon the right decisions being made that night. The good citizens listened in awe as William Morris threatened, bullied and cajoled, telling them of the growing world that was just beyond their sights. Trade. Commerce. Industry. The men leaned forward, no longer afraid, but now suddenly eager to touch this glorious future that shimmered before them. Their leader exhorted them to reach forward and reach deep.

And when the meeting adjourned, the newly formed Tay Navigation Company, of which William Morris was president, had sold nearly all of its available stock. Improvements of the Tay River between Perth and the Rideau Canal for commercial navigation could now begin in earnest.

∾

"Dear Sirs," Donald Fraser's pen scratched across the parchment, his agitation blotting the rough surface. A log in the open grate sparked, momentarily distracting Fraser from his task. He abruptly stood up and walked over to the fire where he kicked the offending ember back into the fireplace with the toe of his worn boot. Clutching the mantle with both hands, he stared down into the fire. A gust of October wind rattled the window panes and pushed a ball of smoke back down the chimney and up into Fraser's face.

"Up in smoke," Fraser coughed, backing away from the hearth. "That's my political career if I can't get someone in York to listen to the truth, instead of more of Morris' damn lies."

It had been a difficult fall for the veteran of the Battle of Chrysler's Farm. Elected to the Legislative Assembly in 1830 and again that year, 1832, together with his political enemy, William Morris, Fraser feared that he was finally going to lose to his powerfully connected foe. Morris had used every trick in the book to prevent the reform-minded Fraser's election to the second seat in Bathurst District, but twice now he had been thwarted. But Fraser was afraid that although Morris had failed to defeat him at the polls, he was finally going to succeed by destroying Fraser's career and reputation.

Fraser smiled as he remembered his election victory seven months before.

His opponent was Colonel Alexander McMillan, an insecure man who was only running because Morris wanted a malleable seat mate in York. McMillan had fought with Fraser at Chrysler's Farm, but McMillan was definitely Morris' man. During the speeches, Fraser had acquitted himself well, he thought, but McMillan, he'd made himself a laughing stock! Just thinking about it made Fraser snort and shake his head with remembered laughter. McMillan couldn't find the end of a sentence if it had a string attached to it! He couldn't follow the course of his own arguments and so ended up falling into a complete blather. The crowds jeered him, but still he soldiered on.

However, despite this poor showing, McMillan continued to lead. Both parties sent out sleighs in all directions right after the speeches to gather up every possible elector. After three days of voting, their efforts showed a victory for Morris and Fraser—a split decision—and that didn't sit well with the Morris camp.

The leading members of the Morris faction were very easy to identify in Perth. They were prosperous, Tories and all directors of the Tay Navigation Company; Colonel McMillan was the treasurer.

In 1831, construction had begun on the canal that would link Perth to the almost completed Rideau Canal and important markets in New York and Montreal, but it was constantly beset with financial difficulties. In January 1832, Morris had successfully petitioned the Executive Council in York to grant the company Cockburn Island, a swampy area in the middle of town that was used for public events like militia training and agricultural fairs. Part of it, Morris maintained, would be excavated for a turning basin, and the Tay Navigation Company would sell off the remainder in lots to help finance the entire project.

Some lots were sold at a public auction on April twenty-first, 1832, but only £300 was raised. Hardly enough to keep the directors in brandy, Fraser grunted to himself. But the people of Perth were finally growing wary of the promises of the Tay Navigation Company. First Morris had played fast and loose with cost projections and now he was trying to sell lots, many of which were currently under water. Promises that this would not be the case once the basin was built did not convince many to purchase now. In true Perth fashion, they were content to wait.

In September, the company obtained a £1,000 loan from the Bank of Upper Canada to finance the basin, but it was turning out to be a wet autumn and construction was being deferred 'til spring. Fraser also noted how a number of the directors held lands close to the projected wharves and basin, which would, naturally, increase in value in the near future.

Fraser, and just about everyone else in town who was not connected to the Morris banditti, had every reason to believe that the directors had benefitted personally from those few lots on Cockburn Island that had been sold. It was no longer public land, much to the annoyance of said public, but Tay Navigation Company property, ergo the directors' property. Fraser supported improved public works but felt that these lots should have been ceded to impartial magistrates to hold in trust; any proceeds from their sale would then be invested in the company to be used for bridges and better navigation.

Fraser felt duty-bound to report these perceived misappropriations of public funds and property, which brought him to this letter. His face burning from the heat of the fire, he returned to his desk and took up his pen again.

"Forty lots, valued for sale at £2,500, which, if all sold, could net Morris and his cronies personal profits as high as twenty per cent! And this is permitted under the company's charter!" The very thought of this made Fraser's blood boil as his arguments to the Executive Council burned into the parchment.

His name signed, Fraser laid down his pen, flexed his cramped fingers and removed his signet ring. As the hot wax dripped onto the folded letter, Fraser paused with his ring held above the slowly congealing red globule. With a sudden movement, he rammed his ring into the wax, sealing irrevocably his political future.

"I knew Fraser would cause us trouble if he was re-elected."

Morris' fist crashed down on the table causing the other members of the Tay Navigation Company to start. The sole item on the day's agenda—a letter from York—was pinned beneath Morris' wrath.

"We must do something immediately to keep the Executive Council from making further inquiries and removing their support from this very necessary project. Damn Fraser and his interfering ways."

Each man round the table silently and frantically searched his mind for a way out of this dilemma. Fraser's letter of complaint to the Executive Council alleging misconduct on the part of the Tay Navigation Company could ruin everything. Despite setbacks caused by the weather, there was no reason to doubt that the much anticipated Tay Canal would be completed within the year. And with the recent opening of the Rideau Canal, each director saw a prosperous future unfolding before him. The Tay and Rideau Canals would provide a reliable, safe, inexpensive highway for exporting the wealth—their wealth—of local farms, mills and forests and importing highly prized manufactured goods. Just think, they could even furnish their homes properly. No more would their wives be forced to ask guests to bring their own chairs whenever they came to dine.

A creaking chair caused Morris to snap his eyes towards the offending noise. Roderick Matheson, Quarter-Master of the Glengarry Fencibles (Light Infantry) during the war, merchant, militia officer and probably the most influential man in Perth after Morris, had leaned forward to pick up the letter. "It seems to me," he began casually, "that we have two problems and they can both be solved with the well-aimed casting of a single stone."

Morris' eyes silently demanded that Matheson continue. All others' pleaded that Matheson present a viable solution.

"Fraser has been making a nuisance of himself," Matheson began. "Firstly, he was elected, denying the Legislative Assembly an able servant," he nodded towards McMillan who was nervously fingering the pages of the company's ledger. "Then he started interfering needlessly in the affairs of the company, when we all know that improved navigation and the construction of wharves will only benefit everyone in Perth and the surrounding townships."

"Get to the point, man," barked an impatient Morris.

Ignoring Morris' impatience, Matheson calmly continued.

"So, it seems that it would be in the public interest to unseat Fraser from the Assembly."

"But he was duly elected," someone sputtered. "We're saddled with him until the next election, which is years away."

"Ah, but I think that there are some questions regarding his eligibility to hold office." Matheson pulled out a folded piece of paper from inside his coat. "It appears that Mr Fraser does not meet the land ownership requirements for sitting in the Legislative Assembly. On his nomination papers," and here he referred to the letter in his hand, "he claims to possess, in the township of Gloucester, lot twenty-nine, sixth concession and lot fifteen, fifth concession, and in the township of Lanark, east lot two, fifth concession."

"But that is public knowledge," ventured McMillan defensively.

"Yes, but what is not public knowledge is that Fraser only holds a location ticket on the first lot—which can be cancelled at any time by the surveyor-general. The second lot is half vacant and half located to someone else who has yet to receive patent for it, and the third lot was a clergy reserve that was sold, but not to Fraser.

"So, gentlemen, it appears that Mr Fraser has falsely represented himself to the people of Lanark and we must not waste any time bringing this to the attention of the Executive Council."

"I would be pleased to support you in your petition to the Assembly," Anthony Leslie quickly volunteered. Murmurs of self-righteous approval rippled around the table.

"Well, that's all very well and fine," began McMillan, "but I don't understand why . . . I mean how . . . I mean Fraser . . . we can't let him get away with . . . what about the damage . . . what about me?"

"What are you babbling about, man?" barked Morris, his pleasure at the anticipation of deposing Fraser already spreading across his face.

"The shares . . . I mean the lots . . . I mean the finances . . ."

"I think he's referring to the Executive Council's inquiries into the disposition of Cockburn Island," interpreted Dr Reade, as he duly noted the proceedings in the minute book.

"Hah!" harumphed Morris. "You leave the Executive Council to me. I will point out to them that the Tay Canal is impossible without outside investment, and that many in Perth—meaning Fraser—have never to this hour afforded the slightest assistance to the company, which by perseverance in the face of almost insurmountable difficulties has enhanced the value of property at Perth to an incredible amount. In fact," Morris mused, warming to his theme, "is it not far preferable to have a navigation and dock such as will be open for public use before this time twelve month, than to see the trade of the town diverted to the banks of the Rideau?" He leaned forward as if addressing the Executive Council directly. "And then leaving Cockburn Island in a state of nature for the accommodation of a cattle fair which, in place of being there, would in all likelihood have assembled at some other place of trade and commerce?"

"Hear, hear!" the directors approved, thumping the table.

Encouraged by this support for his arguments to secure the Executive Council's continued backing for the project, Morris jumped up from the table and began pacing back and forth across the tiny room in an attempt to keep up with his reasoning.

"I will also deny that I or any other director," he momentarily glanced at the fascinated men before him, "benefitted personally from the sale of lots. In fact, so wholly groundless is this insinuation that I defy not only Mr Fraser," his voice rising in indignation, "but the entire community to show that one single farthing from the lots in question ever came into my hands or afforded me, directly or indirectly, the smallest pecuniary advantage. I shall ask Mr Fraser," he slapped his palms onto the table and thrust his chin forward, "to prove that any of us has received one penny for services on behalf of the company. In fact, I shall encourage Mr Fraser and others like him to become stockholders, as money is still needed for these most important of public works." Morris almost crowed with delight at how neatly he had turned the onus on his foe.

"And, of course, this response will be delivered after Matheson and Leslie have delivered their petition to the

Assembly. The scribbled rantings of a discredited and unseated member will, naturally, be quickly discounted."

Morris sat down, congratulations ringing in his ears, and coldly smiled.

∽

A large assembly buzzed indignantly in the taproom of Cross' Hotel. News that Fraser had been unseated from the Legislative Assembly on a technicality had flown back to Perth. A by-election had been called for January second, and Fraser's many, and ever increasing, supporters had quickly called this meeting to formalize his nomination. There would be no slip-ups this time. Proof of land ownership had been duly confirmed by the proper authorities, and not even King William himself could deny Fraser's eligibility to sit as a member of the Legislative Assembly for Upper Canada. Annoyance at Morris' high-handed ways had now grown to disgust, and the crowd cheered when Fraser finally entered the packed room.

It took some time for Fraser to reach the bar from which he would deliver his nomination speech. Everyone wanted to shake his hand and congratulate him for the stand he'd taken against Morris. Although the Executive Council had seen no reason for recommending any change in the disposition of Cockburn Island, it was generally agreed that Morris had used his considerable power in getting the Tay Navigation Company whitewashed. Local opinion rose steadily against him all through the month of December.

"Gentlemen," Fraser shouted so as to be heard above the exuberance surrounding him. "Gentlemen! Friends," a great cheer erupted and it was several Huzzas! before Fraser could again speak.

"Friends. We are gathered here in the warm surroundings of Mr Cross' fine establishment," he raised his hand to gently silence those who would now salute the landlord, "because of the intrigues of a faction who took advantage of a quibble of law. Now, we don't need to go into details here, but this is not the first time earnest, hard-working members of this community have been subject to this `Timothy's' perfidy."

"Trucebreaker! False accuser! Blasphemer!" shouted some-one from the back of the room to a chorus of hisses at this bib-lical reference to Fraser's self-righteous foe.

Fraser continued, barely acknowledging the interruption which had distracted a few of his more zealous supporters and threatened to turn his nomination into a revival meeting.

"In fact, Reverend Bell here," all eyes turned towards the dour Scotsman who had strategically placed himself so that anyone wishing to replenish his tankard would have to pass under the disapproving gaze of the Presbyterian minister, "was once the recipient of an `anonymous' letter," hoots greet-ed this insinuation, "written in a feigned hand, that tried to involve this noble man of the cloth in a quarrel our friend `Timothy' was having with the Kingston postmaster.

"It seems that our opponent has a habit of manipulating the truth for his own good. And he has been enfranchised to enact on our behalf? For to quote the apostle Paul, also in a letter, but to our `friend's' namesake, `But we know that the law is good, if a man use it lawfully.'" Derisive whoops supported this comparison, and Fraser let it ride while he satisfied him-self that William Tully, the editor of the *Constitution*, was prop-erly recording the proceedings. And as the din began to ebb, he made his final thrust. "So, tell me," he asked, all innocence, "just who is the honourable man?"

The room erupted again with loud huzzas, and tankards were refilled in a chorus of toasts and cheers for their chosen man.

TO THE
ELECTORS
OF THE
County of Lanark

Gentlemen,

With feelings of the utmost indignation I have perused an infamous production signed Z. To read it is to detest it, and look with scorn upon the vile and slanderous author. Shame and everlasting contempt upon the wretch who could fabricate such an abominable tissue of prevarication.

Infamous as it is; low, vulgar and false as it is; it is nothing to the character of the vile man whose grovelling imagination could prompt him to pen such a composition of lies! To read it, to blame it, (as Timothy's brother says) and to repudiate the polluted sink of unworthiness from which this sluggish stench of vituperation has emanated, is the plan of adoption to every reasonable man who is untainted by prejudice, and uninfluenced by the corruption of an interested, undermining and time-serving party. Gentlemen, you know that party: beware of those who compose it.

Timothy, Timothy, and Caleb Quotem, ye base assassins of reputation, ye foul-mouth stabbers in the dark; your time-worn masks no longer conceal the deformities of your hypocritical features. Ye are both well known. This production of Z shows the long-existing friendship which Caleb has always had towards Mr. Fraser. Gentlemen, Mr. F. is an honest man, and the venom of a miserable tool like Z can do him no harm.

Gentlemen, come boldly forward on the day of Election, and with one accord re-elect the man of your choice, and the friend of the people, in spite of the aristocratic cowardly opposition, and its jesuitical leader, Timothy.

Gentlemen, your Servant and fellow elector,
A HATER OF HYPOCRITES
Lanark, 29th Dec., 1832[1]

William Morris tore the handbill from the tree and crumpled it savagely in his hands. His dark eyes quickly took in the crowd gathering around the hastily erected hustings. Colourful bunting fluttered from the leafless trees, making them look like gaudily dressed matrons at a fall fair. The liquor was circulating freely, and minor tussles were already punctuating the throng. Morris' eye traced a trail of blood to a man sitting dazed on the side of the road. His nose was broken, and he seemed impervious both to the pain and the barrage of abuse being flung at him by his irate wife. There'd be a lot more blood spilt before the victor was declared, Morris thought abstractedly.

A blast of January's icy breath snapped to attention a sole white flag. Its starkness was further emphasized by the black gibbet painted on it. Hanging from the rope was a large Z. Morris scowled, then shivered as fingers of cold reached inside his collar. Dr George Hume Reade came up alongside Morris holding a copy of the same handbill that Morris still held clenched in his fist.

"We seem to be experiencing some opposition."

"Have you prepared your speech?"

"Yes," Reade replied confidently.

"Well, let's begin."

Reade and Morris made their way through the election revellers to the platform. Morris ignored the anonymous jests that followed him through the crowd identifying him as Z. There was no proof that he had authored the liberally circulated handbill abusing Fraser, and he had more important things on his mind than acknowledging the hecklers.

Their way was suddenly blocked by two men, whose only means of support was each other and even that was dubious on the very icy streets. "Docshter Reade," slurred one. "On the recom . . . the recom . . . the advish of Father McDonnell, I be honoured to cast my vote for you in this . . . in this . . . exershize in democracy—hic—Even though you are a Gawd-damned Orangeman!"

The two then made to hoist Reade onto their shoulders, but they quickly slipped and were soon rolling in the snow in drunken laughter. Morris put his hand on Reade's shoulder and pushed him towards the platform. Reade turned his head to face Morris.

"Good work, Morris. With the Catholic vote, my election is assured."

Morris merely grunted as he cast his eyes around the crowd. His men were busy unloading more barrels of whisky and ale to the grateful electorate. Fraser's men were doing the same, but he noticed with some unease the large number of Orangemen accepting the Presbyterian's largesse.

The returning officer, J.F.W. Berford, was attempting to demand some order so that the election could begin. The two opposing factions had been hard at work scouring the countryside for any and all possible voters. The promise of free liquor had been enough to lure them away from their hearths on this bitter winter's day, and most were already feeling the whisky's warmth.

A sleigh bore down upon the hustings, scattering those still sober enough to notice. The clearly intoxicated driver was slashing his whip at everything but the horses, which strained frantically to flee the madman at the reins. They saw a break in the crowd and lurched towards it, throwing the driver backwards onto his seat and momentarily knocking the wind from him. He let the reins fall. Free from restraint, the horses raced for freedom. Suddenly, someone noticed that a man—an Irishman, Noonan, someone said—was standing right in their path, completely unaware of his danger! Other voices soon turned into screams of horror for the fallen man lying face down in the snow. Blood dribbled from his grotesquely twisted jaws. Berford, who was responsible for the smooth running of the election, quickly and calmly summoned medical attention for the man and then took advantage of the lull in the fighting to read the writ.

Once the legalities had been observed, authorizing the election of a member from Lanark to the Legislative Assembly of Upper Canada, Berford asked for the names of any and all candidates wishing to run. Only Fraser and Reade's names were put forward. Berford then asked that each man deliver a speech for the consideration of the voters assembled.

Dr Reade went first. He reminded the assembled that he too was a veteran of the Napoleonic Wars, in which he had served as an apothecary. Like many of them gathered there today, he had seen too much horror during the years of war, and that now, in peace, he was dedicated to realizing the opportunities found in a new land. But Reade, while skilled in the elegant manoeuvrings of the back room, was a neophyte in the open political warfare of the hustings. He had a difficult time making himself heard above the incessant and extremely voluble heckling. His tormenters—Irishmen—were easily identified as friends of Fraser, and they found Reade an easy target for abuse. Their shrapnel of gibe ranged from innuendo to insult and they soon had Reade's speech shot to shreds. Desperate, Reade righteously exclaimed that he was a man independent in his circumstances and honest in his principles. So ludicrous was this statement that, for blocks around, the streets exploded with mocking laughter—even from his supporters—forcing Reade, red-faced and flustered, to take his seat.

Fraser, however, found inspiration in the occasion. He was a man reborn. He showed no sign at all of the troubled individual who, only a scant three months before, had faced political ruin. He played with the assembled, juggling their taunts and torments with the skill of a circus performer. The crowd loved it. And when he declared that he had been disqualified by the intrigues of a faction that had taken advantage of a law quibble, it was all Berford could do to prevent the crowd from chairing Fraser right then and there.

"As the two candidates have now stated their platforms," Berford began, straining his voice to be heard above the cheers, "I ask all freehold citizens to divide: those in support of Dr Reade to stand on my left and those in support of Mr Fraser on my right."

It was very apparent, even to a blind man, that the majority of men there favoured the return of Fraser to his rightful seat in the legislature. The late afternoon sun was beginning to set and some Irish had lit a bonfire to start the next stage of the celebrations. However, before Berford could declare Fraser a winner, Morris stepped forward.

"I demand a poll."

For three days, the polls remained open as each side worked night and day to collect supporters. Word had spread quickly of Morris' ongoing attempts to discredit Fraser, and more and more made the perilous trek into Perth to declare their vote for Fraser. On the fourth day of January, 1833, Dr Reade finally conceded defeat. Celebrations were renewed in earnest, and a thoroughly vindicated Fraser was chaired around the town in grand style. Revellers lit bonfires on every corner, and liquor ran in the streets like water.

And from his window overlooking Gore Street, William Morris scowled before snapping his curtains shut against the Methodist who preached from the book of Timothy alone in the snow below:

"For the love of money is the root of all evil: which while some coveted after, they have erred from the faith, and pierced themselves through with many sorrows."

William Morris (1786-1858) as photographed in 1850. Morris was born in Paisley, Scotland, and emigrated to Brockville in 1801. After fighting in the War of 1812, where he was present at the taking of Ogdensburg, he moved to Perth and opened its first store, on the south shore of the Tay. Here he slept on a buffalo robe behind the counter–a piece of bark straddling two barrels. One of Perth's more influential citizens, he enjoyed a successful political and business career. First elected to the Legislative Assembly for Upper Canada in 1820, he eventually rose to the offices of Receiver-General (1844-46) and President of the Executive Council (1846-48) and was a founder of Queen's University. Morris was a strong advocate of the Church of Scotland and fought hard to have it recognized alongside the Church of England as an established church.
Credit: Queen's University Archives.

Credit: Perth Museum.

AN ENTERPRISING VENTURE

The weather-beaten sailor looked at the unfinished vessel before him. The ugly scars that marred Captain William Richard's leathery skin would have been enough to discourage many in the happy crowd gathering by the new Tay turning basin, but his rigid stance and stern countenance dissuaded even the most exuberant from approaching him. The sailor had come a long way since signing on as a cabin boy aboard a British man-of-war at the age of twelve. He had sailed all around the world meeting success and failure head-on in both war and peace, but he thought he had left it all behind when he and his wife moved to Perth a few years before. What could be further from a seafaring life than a small brick cottage on fourteen acres in an army settlement, thousands of miles from the sea?

But the Duke of Wellington—hero of Waterloo—had devised an elaborate scheme to protect the British North American colonies against future attacks from the Americans to the south. Military settlements at Perth, Richmond and Lanark would provide the trained men when it was time to march again; extensive and impregnable defences being constructed in Kingston would repel the invaders and a navigable inland waterway being dug and blasted along the Rideau and Cataraqui waterways would safely connect Montreal and Kingston.

This canal was going to be big. The Royal Engineers were building locks that could accommodate steamships more than a hundred feet long, thirty feet wide and drawing five feet of water. Struggling industrialists saw a golden opportunity for trade with this new canal, and there was fierce campaigning by every community within rowing distance to have the route include it. Perth was one of the unsuccessful candidates, but that didn't stop the town fathers, led by the political and industrial force of William Morris, from forming their own company to build their own navigable waterway that would link them with the Rideau Canal.

And what was a navigation company without a flagship? An enterprise of this stature deserved a vessel to ply the waters of the new Tay and Rideau Canals, importing fine merchandise from far-off places and exporting Perth's cheeses, whiskies, timber, grains and woollen goods to various and sundry ports beyond. So, while locks were being excavated, dams erected and channels cleared along the silt-clogged Tay River, a search was launched to find a shipbuilder for the Tay Navigation Company's *Enterprise*.

Captain William Richards had barely lived to see his second birthday, let alone grown up to sail the seven seas. While still just an infant in Wexford, Ireland, both his mother and his father had been brutally piked to death in their own home during the violent uprising at Vinegar Hill in 1798. Young William's nurse managed to save his life from the warring factions only by fleeing with him and claiming him for her own. He escaped death yet again, and many times over, during the War of 1812 and, after the war, in numerous skirmishes with pirates and slavers.

Eventually he left the Royal Navy and invested in a trading schooner, which he sailed between the Bay of Fundy and the West Indies. Captain Richards expanded his interests to shipbuilding and was soon sailing his own brig, the *William and Mary*, on the profitable West Indies run. This comfortable life may have continued forever, but Captain Richards lost everything—ship and cargo—in a hurricane during a return voyage. In fact, he and his crew barely escaped with their own lives. They managed to free a small boat from their capsized and quickly sinking ship, which eventually took them to shore. The *William and Mary's* cargo of molasses was uninsured, which left the old sailor with only enough money to buy a small farm in an inland settlement, far from the perils of the sea.

But that quiet life lasted only until he met William Morris, president of the Tay Navigation Company. The previous September of 1832, he had been drawn back into the shipping life when the Tay Navigation Company hired him to build and captain the steamship *Enterprise*. All winter he worked on her, and on April third, 1833, she was launched. It wasn't quite the official launch, as the *Enterprise* was far from complete, but she was seaworthy enough to sail down to Brockville to receive her engine.

This would be a safe commission, thought Captain Richards, perfect for a retired sea dog who had been maybe just a bit too hasty in turning his back so firmly on the only life he had ever known. It was little better than barging, and the Rideau was a tame pussycat compared to the snarling Atlantic.

The launching of the *Enterprise* took on the appearance of a holiday. For many people, this was the first time they had ever attended such an event. And the excitement was compounded by the hopes that this was just the beginning of a new era of development for the tiny community. True, the locks of the Tay Canal were not quite finished yet (there had been some financial difficulties and inclement weather), and they were smaller than those on the Rideau (which could be restricting), but the Rideau had been in operation since last summer, and it was only a matter of time before the Tay, too, was bustling with trading vessels of all descriptions.

Captain Richards boarded his steamboat. A great cheer rose from the shore as the oxen managed to tug the *Enterprise* into motion. Slowly, but with dignity, the half-finished steamer passed through the Drummond and Beckwith Street swing-bridges. A gaggle of young boys followed her progress, bumping into themselves and others as they tumbled along the canal bank. Things came to a confused and momentary halt while planks were hastily removed from the low Craig Street bridge so the steamboat could pass, but soon the oxen driver was whipping his beasts into motion, and the *Enterprise* found her momentum again.

It took about three months for the *Enterprise* to reach Brockville, but reach it she did and, in fact, she made it back to the Rideau Lakes before freeze-up.

It was another fine spring day that saluted the *Enterprise* when she came home to Perth on May first, 1834. It had been a bit of an effort getting through the still-not-quite-completed locks on the Tay, but all was in readiness in Perth. The Perth Artillery stood at attention on the new Drummond Street bridge and fired off several rounds in salute as the *Enterprise* sailed into the basin. The crowds who, more than a year ago, had seen her off were there to greet her return. All day, the people of Perth inspected the freshly painted steamer, with its fine promenade deck and other pleasing additions. It was a good-sized vessel with about thirty cabins and room for a hundred steerage passengers and seventy-five tons of cargo. Congratulations were handed all round to members of the Tay Navigation Company, and profits were being calculated as each load was carried aboard for the first transhipment to Kingston.

Captain Richards and his cargo set sail the next day. A small party of shareholders elected to speed the *Enterprise* on her way and joined the captain for the short leg to Dowson's Lock at Jebb's Creek. The enthusiasm of the morning soon began to sputter as the original eight o'clock sailing time was delayed until ten. Finally underway, Captain Richards struggled to maintain his course in the narrow river's stubborn current. There were difficulties passing through the first bridge and a further delay while a barge in tow loaded with staves was securely fastened. At last, the journey could begin. Cheers were raised and greetings extended to the occasional urchin found fishing along the river bank. It was a fine spring day, as can only be found in May, and the passengers all gathered on the promenade deck to admire the passing scenery. An uncomfortable hush came over the assembled when they neared the spot where poor Robert Lyon had been killed in the tragic duel with John Wilson, only a year before.

Their respectful observance was suddenly shattered when overhanging branches from the trees along the shore swept all the passengers on the promenade deck to the floor. All of a sudden, Captain Richards was yelling at his crew. The *Enterprise* had come to a crunching halt. An inspection of the grounded steamer produced a fairly extensive list of damages: shattered railing, broken flagstaff, toppled stove-pipes, a clogged engine pipe, and several bruised passengers. This was indeed a cursed spot.

Spirits were definitely low until the captain ordered that the bar be opened, much to the shock and disapproval of the Reverend William Bell. Never would the Presbyterian minister have allowed William Morris to talk him into buying his two ten-pound shares if he had known that intoxicating liquors would be sold on board. He also learned that the *Enterprise* would sail on the sabbath!

An hour later, more than four hours after they had been scheduled to embark but with most passengers in improved cheer, the *Enterprise* finally steamed out of sight of the steeples of Perth, never to return.

In fact, no steamship ever again made it past the first set of tiny, poorly constructed locks at Pike Falls.[1] The Tay was just too shallow, too weedy, too treacherous. It became more cost-effective to tranship goods onto barges like the *Jolly Brewer, Pride of Perth, The Old Countryman* and the *Perseverance,* at the Perth Landing on Stonehouse Point, just at the mouth of the Tay. Steady oxen would then laboriously tow the barges up to Perth, heavily laden with everything from beds to sickles and books to nails, against the Tay's, at times, strong and wilful current.

Meanwhile, the *Enterprise* endeavoured to live up to its name.

Captain Richards soon established a routine, shipping goods from Bytown to Perth to Kingston and back, docking at the Perth Landing once a week, sometimes twice. He carried whisky, cider, tobacco, paint, shovels, fruit trees, flour, potash, pork, household furnishings, tea, ploughs, molasses, sugar, raisins, soap, ginger, wine, furs, candles . . . and whatever else people needed or wanted to trade.[2]

[1] Port Elmsley.
[2] Tay Navigation Company Ledger 13 May 1834-17 November 1835.

However, while goods may have been safely delivered to their destination, people weren't always. The treatment passengers received on the *Enterprise's* maiden voyage seems to have to set the tone for the two seasons the steamboat plied the Rideau. On one particularly disastrous voyage, one disgruntled passenger wrote:

A more uncomfortable situation I could not have been placed in. What with the heat, dirt, noise, mosquitoes and drunkards, I never met the equal.[3]

Two days into the trip, the *Enterprise* broke down (a frequent occurrence), and Captain Richards set off on foot to Kingston for assistance. There were insufficient provisions on board for this enforced delay, and the passengers who had been left behind were soon forced to fish for their supper. They also attempted to capture a deer that had come down to the shore, but failed. Things came to a serious head, however, when the cook mutinied.

It was a load of potash that finally did the *Enterprise* in. Early in December 1835, the *Enterprise* became stuck in the ice at Black Rapids on her way to Montreal. She wintered there, and when spring finally unleashed the Rideau's pent-up energies, the enraged river used its fury to pound all life out of the unfortunate steamer.

And so ended the *Enterprise* that wasn't. It also pretty well sums up the entire history of the Tay Navigation Company and the Tay Canal. Lack of capital, feuds (that's another story, or four) and a poorly designed canal soon reduced the private waterway to a timber chute for the great stands of oak north of Perth.

The hapless steamer's engines were sold to George Buchanan and Company in Arnprior and provided the power for a steamer of the same name on Chats Lake.

And Captain William Richards? Well, he captained the *George Buchanan* for a couple of years and then retired for good—to live out his years in his little brick cottage on fourteen acres of dry land near an army settlement, thousands of miles from the sea.

---

[3] "Sound of Her Whistle," Parks Canada, 1979.

The *Pilot* by George Seton (1844). Against initial orders from London, Colonel By opted to build the locks on the Rideau Canal large enough to accommodate the new steamboats. Unfortunately, the directors of the Tay Navigation Company did not follow suit. By's proved to be the wiser decision and soon the Rideau teemed with commercial and passenger vessels like the *Pilot*, while only barges towed by oxen could safely navigate the canal up to Perth. Although less arduous than travelling by land, the early steamers offered their fares rough passage, including crude wooden bunks on which to sleep.
Credit: Public Archives of Canada.

Downstream from the Craig Street Bridge showing the old Tay Canal towpath in 1903.
Credit: Parks Canada, Rideau Canal.

Steamer *Aileen* on Tay Canal near Perth, c. 1890. Although this postcard depicts the Tay after it was rebuilt and enlarged in the 1880s, the scene is very similar to that which would have seen the *Enterprise* off when it sailed from Perth nearly sixty years before.
Credit: Parks Canada, Rideau Canal

THE VISIT

There was excitement everywhere you went.

Men buzzed, women fluttered and children just couldn't stay still. All was in a flurry as housewives shooed the first autumn leaves from their doorsteps and then dared the maples to drop any more. Stable hands bowed and scraped in awkward step with their skittish horses and dogs raced through the streets, chasing litter into hiding. Regimental finery was pressed into shape and brightly coloured ostrich feathers were coaxed to stand tall, just one more time.

What started out as an occasional ahem, soon grew into an epidemic of throat clearing. Entire households were commanded to listen to revision after revision of welcoming speeches, introductory speeches, congratulatory speeches, self-deprecating speeches, rousing speeches, boring speeches and thank-you speeches in preparation for The Visit.

For the Lieutenant-Governor of Upper Canada, Sir John Colborne, was coming to Perth!

Not since the Duke of Richmond's visit in 1819—some sixteen years before—had such an exalted personage deigned to grace this small community with his presence. Although it was the capital of the District of Bathurst—and the administrative, judicial and social centre for the interior—it was remote and, until the recent completion of the Rideau and Tay Canals, difficult to reach. So, when the Reverend Michael Harris, on alt from his visit to Toronto to see the bishop, let it be known that His Excellency the Lieutenant-Governor, was planning to visit Perth on Wednesday, the thirtieth day of September, in the Year of Our Lord, eighteen hundred and thirty-five, well . . . you can just imagine the stir it created.

Such fluffing and puffing, primping and crimping, sighing and prying as to who would be wearing what and standing where. The town fathers gathered at the courthouse, armed with briefings from their wives, to draw up the agenda for the lieutenant-governor's brief stay. Not since the Battle of Chrysler's Farm had many of these men been challenged to devise such delicate strategies. Tactical placement of magistrates, militia officers, merchants and men of the cloth—not to mention their wives and daughters—took on the importance of a full-scale campaign. Oh yes, the militia too was mustered—some 900 strong—and charged with the polishing of boots, buttons and bayonets and then drilled and re-drilled in anticipation of the viceregal review.

The Day finally arrived.

All was in readiness. Every last man, woman and child had been squeezed into their Sunday best. And so much gold braid! The September sun was so dazzled by it all that it was forced occasionally to shield its eyes behind a gauzy wisp of cloud. Precious jewels winked coyly at the sparkles rippling across the Tay, and a rainbow of silks and satins floated into position on the cool autumn breezes.

Ta-rum. Ta-rum. Ta-rum-tum-tum.

The militia, all sprigged out, marched briskly up Gore Street with muskets oiled and uniforms brushed. The artillery splintered off to array itself on the new Drummond Street bridge over the Tay, while the remainder arranged itself for inspection on Cockburn Island. A fast rider had been stationed at Oliver's Ferry to watch for the arrival of the lieutenant-governor's party, and all peered anxiously down Gore Street in nervous anticipation.

A swirl of dust was seen off in the distance. Everyone rustled into place, and the militia came to attention. The excitement was palpable. Then the swirl grew into a cloud. A child squealed. The cloud took on dimensions. A tightly corseted matron swooned. A horse and rider came into view. The militia captain poised his smouldering punk above the cannon's touch-hole. It was . . . it was . . . an itinerant pedlar.

Once this disappointment had been hustled away, everyone reassembled in ready position.

And waited.

And waited.

And waited.

Until, by sunset, mothers could no longer keep their children in order, and there were no more soldiers to fill the holes left by fainting comrades. By ones and twos, the good people of Perth began drifting away on mutters of chores to be done and fires to be lit. It was a sombre mood that gently covered the unfulfilled dreams that night.

BOOM! BOOM! BOOM BOOM BOOM!!!

Whazat?

Tousled heads burst through shuttered windows in time to discard the rumour of earthquake and grasp the intelligence that the lieutenant-governor had finally arrived and was even now crossing the new bridge! Legs were thrust hastily into crumpled breeches and figures crushed into bent stays so carelessly tossed aside only a few short hours before. All pretence of order and discipline was abandoned in the wild scramble to secure a position before the unexpected approach. There was much shoving and pushing to be the first to see Sir John.

Which one was he?

BOOM!

The sound of cannon recoiled into the confused crowd, scattering it under available cover. As the smoke cleared, several saw a tangle of arms and legs windmilling it into the lanes and alleyways off Gore Street. Where was the lieutenant-governor? Was he injured? Was he killed? Were the Americans attacking?

Everyone felt arms and legs and discovered that no bones had been broken and no blood had been spilt. As they gathered at the bridge, they noticed that a gun had indeed been fired, but there was no armada sinking in the Tay Basin and no dead bodies lying prostrate in the early morning sun. And what was even more disappointing, there was no viceregal party on progress to meet the good citizens of Perth.

It soon became very apparent that the cannon had been fired by some rogues who had removed it from the safety of Mr Graham's yard so as to wreak mischief. So, amidst grumblings at the irresponsibility of youth, the townsfolk returned to their homes to break their fast. Like the dreams of an aging spinster, their hopes of recognition were carefully packed away once more.

Life soon reverted to normal. Millers milled, farmers farmed, blacksmiths smithed and brewers brewed. Attention turned to the fair, scheduled for the following Tuesday. It rained all that day, turning roads into rivers and the fairgrounds into a quagmire, but that didn't prevent a tremendous amount of business being conducted in the cake and beer shops and the apple and gingerbread stalls.

Friday, the ninth day of October rose fresh and clear—one of those rare October days when you feel that Mother Nature has repented and will, just this once, forget about winter this year. It was a relief after all the rain and cold to feel the warmth of the sun on your face and firm ground beneath your feet. The maid was hanging up the laundry at the St George Hotel when she saw a small party come to a stop in the yard. All were strangers, which was not unusual at an inn, and they looked dusty and travel-worn, which again was not unusual. She didn't pay them much attention until she saw young Cross, the innkeeper's son, burst out the front door only moments after the new guests had entered.

It was the lieutenant-governor!

No explanation was given as to why he had come now and not before, nor was there time to waste worrying about it. The important thing was that He was here. Sir John Colborne had come!

A special meeting was called at the courthouse, where the old speeches were dusted off and reviewed as to their suitability at this late date. The magistrates prepared a new address and had it sent around town by Mr James Young, the gaoler, for signatures from all the necessary magistrates, etc.— but only by those of a purely *British* nature, the *Bathurst*

Courier sniffed. As they were hastily penning their names, they were told—along with their wives and daughters—to gather at the courthouse at twelve o'clock for official presentation to the lieutenant-governor.

And then it was over.

Everyone who was anyone had been presented to the lieutenant-governor at the courthouse. Fresh cravats hastily tied into intricate knots and paisley shawls draped over everyday dresses—there wasn't time to air out the silks and satins—were the only outward trappings signifying the importance of the event.

Sheriff Powell had read the address to His Excellency, expressing the town's Approbation of His Conduct in the Administration of the Government of this Province and returning thanks to him for having Honoured them with a Visit. His Excellency's answer to this address was short but pleasing and satisfactory.

Sir John then walked to the top of the English Church hill to review the town. The artillery had been hastily mustered to the bridge below where they smartly fired a salute to His Excellency and then executed several exercises for his pleasure. There was more than the occasional muffled snort when Sir John congratulated them on their order and the well-regulated discipline with which they did their exercises, as well as the respectful manner in which they conducted themselves on the occasion. For one gun was missing, the one that had been fired the week before. It had been left on the Drummond Street bridge that entire day, in the rain, and had yet to be put back in trim.

Basking in the glow of the lieutenant-governor's praise, the corps then presented a petition to His Excellency, praying that he might be pleased to grant them side arms and ammunition for the purpose of practising more frequently–!–than they had theretofore, and without being put to the disagreeable necessity of going round soliciting powder from the merchants. His Excellency agreed to see to their petition's fulfilment when he returned to the capital.

Then it was a stroll around town to admire its situation and improvements, and gracious thanks to the town fathers for their kind hospitality and attention.

And as Sir John and his entourage were waved out of sight, the Reverend Bell was heard to comment, "Never were people more anxious to recommend themselves to the notice of great men than those holding offices here. This sometimes afforded them an opportunity of making themselves ridiculous."[1]

NOTICES.

St. George Hotel.

THE proprietor of this Hotel wishes to inform his friends & the travelling community in general, that, instead of having left this place, as has been industriously circulated throughout the District, by some designing person, still continues to keep the above establishment, in the same place as formerly where every possible attention will be paid to the convenience and comfort of his Guests. His table is at all times supplied with the best the District can afford, and the Bar stored with Wines and Liquors of the first quality.

He, in conclusion, returns thanks to those who have heretofore favoured him with their patronage, and hopes by unremitted zeal and attention, to merit further favours from them.

WILLIAM CROSS.

Perth, Dec. 22, 1836.

Advertisement from the *Bathurst Courier* for the St George Hotel.

[1] Rev. Wm. Bell Diaries, 1835

St George Hotel, 15 Harvey Street.
Credit: Commonwealth Historic Resource Management

Perth courthouse with cannons. The history of the two three-pound light infantry guns that now guard the Perth courthouse is a mixture of fact and fancy. Cast by Dutch-born master founders Jan and Pieter Verbruggen of the British Royal Brass Foundry in 1775 and 1776, legend has it they were lost by General Burgoyne to the Americans at the Battle of Saratoga in 1777 and then recaptured by the British at the Battle of Chrysler's Farm in 1813. In 1820, Lord Dalhousie, governor-in-chief of the Canadas, ordered that the guns be sent to Perth to "applaud and encourage" the settlement's military spirit and "induce them to form volunteer companies."
Credit: Commonwealth Historic Resource Management

SHILLINGS AND SHINPLASTERS

The warm afternoon sun had lured the fisherman away from his cares and responsibilities to a comfortable hollow in the banks of the Tay River. A five-pound bass dithered just beyond his line, trying to decide whether to snatch the juicy worm or heed the warnings of his schoolmates who trod water safely behind him. Patience . . . patience . . .

Clang! clang! clang! With a guilty jerk, the truant pulled on his line just a moment too soon, scattering the fish into the cool recesses of the river. Clang! clang! clang! The distant bell persisted in its summons. The fisherman scowled back at the interruption and squirmed his way further into the river bank as if he could hide himself away from both searching eyes and calls to duty. The trick was to keep perfectly still.

Soon, the clangs from the meddlesome bell rippled off into silence, and the river smoothed its surface back to reflect its natural calm. The wild flowers nodded drowsily and the soft summer breeze yawned and sighed before settling down to an afternoon's nap in the arms of an overhanging willow tree. Nothing moved.

Snap! Splash! Flop!

The large bass collapsed in the grass beside its unfortunate mates and gaped glassy-eyed at the fisherman, who smiled back with satisfaction as he ever so quietly rebaited his hook.

❧

Old man McFarlane painstakingly totted up the columns of figures in the ledger book. He paused briefly to calculate a rate of exchange, made a small notation in the margin and turned the page. English pounds, American dollars, Spanish pistareens and French crowns–merchants and bankers accepted all currencies as legal tender since Upper Canada had yet to claim one as its own. True, the Bank of Upper Canada issued its own notes, but if a farmer came in to settle his debts with a combination of Spanish and American dollars–especially in coin–no self-respecting shopkeeper would refuse him. And if that farmer needed change, well, the shopkeeper would cut a silver dollar into halves or quarters to balance the account. The government at York, now Toronto, had tried to instil some order into this very unstable economy by passing An Act for the Better Regulation of Currency in 1830, but all that did was to decree that silver coins desecrated to more than one-twenty-fifth of their full weight would no longer be accepted as legal tender. In some ways, barter was easier; in all ways, bookkeeping was difficult.

A happy whistle danced through the window to distract the diligent clerk.

"Damn," he muttered, as he returned to the top of the column to begin the figuring again.

"Ah, McFarlane, have you smelled the roses today? I truly think that this is the finest year for them, although I notice some animal has rearranged the mulch in the bushes over by the fence. I'll have to address that tomorrow."

"Yes, sir," rasped McFarlane in acknowledgement, as he shuffled over to the shelf where the ledgers were kept. "A farmer from the third line of Bathurst arrived earlier. Wanted to . . ."

"Ah, yes–and look what I've caught us for dinner," he interrupted as he proudly raised a string of three fat bass for the old clerk's inspection.

"Very nice, Captain Leslie." McFarlane shuffled back to his stool.

"Nothing like a hot August afternoon for catching a bit of dinner. In all, I'd say it was a very profitable day. How were things here at the bank?"

"As I was saying, sir. A farmer from the third line of Bathurst arrived before. Wanted to make a withdrawal. Rang the bell."

"Oh, yes," recalled the captain. "I vaguely remember hearing something like that. Dashed inconvenient time 'though. I was just about to snag this most succulent bass when that bell came clanging all over the countryside. Well, I'm glad to hear that it was no one important. Anything else?"

"Yes, sir," he wheezed. "I've finished the report for the directors of the Commercial Bank. If you'd care to look it over . . ."

"Yes, yes, of course, McFarlane. But first, let's see if we can find the kitchen maid to clean these fish, and then we'll inform Mrs Leslie of the surprise I've brought for dinner."

Captain Anthony Leslie, retired on half-pay from the Glengarry Fencibles (Light Infantry), had been among the original inhabitants of the Perth Military Settlement when it was established in 1816. He drew, as part of his land grant for loyal service during the War of 1812, a twenty-five acre park on Wilson Street West, just on the limits of the original town. By 1830, he had built a square frame cottage in a small glade of elms and planted roses, his pride and joy.

In 1835, he became the local agent for the Commercial Bank, giving the people of Perth and area a choice in where to secure their money; Roderick Matheson had been appointed agent for the City Bank some time before. These new responsibilities did not interfere much with his established order. In addition to being a farmer and fisherman, he was now a banker—and in that order. He set aside a room in his home for an office, erected a bell so that he could be summoned by anyone wishing to do business and proceeded to carry on pretty much as before. For this, the Commercial Bank paid him $600 a year—an amount which he never did enough business to cover.

"Sir," puffed McFarlane, "did you see the editorial in this week's issue of the *Bathurst Courier*? There are complaints of merchants refusing to receive coppers. Considered spurious. A great inconvenience," he gasped, breathless from this lengthy speech.

"Yes, yes, McFarlane, I agree. But necessary. There are many bad coppers in circulation," declaimed Captain Leslie, "and steps must be taken to prevent the total debasement of currency in this province!"

"But sir," McFarlane drew breath noisily in preparation for his argument. "If I may be so bold. There is confusion. One merchant will take one kind of copper, when another won't. Need consensus. Crisis."

Captain Leslie thought long and hard that night over what his clerk had said. There was no question: the country—the continent—was experiencing a currency crisis. The previous summer, Andrew Jackson, president of the United States, had issued the Specie Circular. It demanded that, henceforth, all purchases of public lands would be paid for in gold or silver. This was an attempt to curb reckless land speculating in that country which had been financed by either easy credit or unsecured bank notes.

This demand for cold, hard cash immediately put a strain on available gold and silver reserves, and caused the American land market to bottom out. By May tenth, 1837, panic had swept the United States, and the banks, saddled with foreclosed mortgages on now worthless properties, suspended all specie payments. Upper and Lower Canada, with no currency to call their own, soon followed suit.

Captain Leslie leaned over the side of his bed, lifted the bed skirt and peered into the dim recesses. He collapsed back onto his pillow and whistled warily through his teeth. The dust bunnies still stood guard. But would that trap door be security enough against a mob of angry clients, determined to retrieve their deposits?

On Sunday morning, Captain Leslie attended church with his wife, this the only occasion for which Mrs Leslie would leave her home. As always, she had dressed herself in the same sensible, although now worn, outfit in which she had arrived as a bride from Kingston. When the captain walked up the aisle to the altar with the collection, he noticed a coupon in amongst the smaller-than-usual assortment of coins: "Good for one shave," it said over the signature of a local barber.

"Hmmm," thought Leslie distractedly. "Worth about three-pence."

The next day, Captain Leslie walked downtown to conduct some business in his capacity as license inspector for stills, innkeepers and shops for Bathurst District. It was a pleasant walk up the long, steady incline of Wilson Street, and he was kept busy acknowledging the many acquaintances heading to and fro on the congested road. At Foster Street, he turned left and plunged into Perth's bustling commercial centre. Fine ladies and their maids sidestepped racing boys and dogs, while horse carts competed with men carrying heavy sacks on their shoulders for space on the narrow streets. And one farmer was trying gamely to drive a herd of cattle down Gore Street to the docks in the Tay Basin, which only added to the seeming chaos. "Well," observed Leslie to his neighbour on the corner, as they waited for the cattle to pass through the intersection of Foster and Gore, "at least he has them under control."

"Yes, and it's a rare thing too," harumphed the man. "Many's a time, especially in winter, these beasts are left to run at will through the town. Their owners are new to farming and know little of their care. They leave them to forage even the little bits of hay that might be dangling from a sleigh or cart!"

The man was obviously warming to a theme, and Leslie did not have time to indulge him now. He searched frantically for a break in the traffic. Finally, the road cleared, and Leslie uttered a hasty agreement as the two of them crossed the street. Nodding politely, he escaped by ducking into the shop of William and John Bell.

After a period of apprenticeship in Perth merchant houses, the twin sons of the Reverend William Bell had opened their own general emporium in 1828 on the south side of Foster Street, between Gore and Drummond. They had been born in London, England, in 1806, but had lived in Perth since the family's arrival in 1817 when they were eleven. Astute businessmen, they had another store in Morphy's Falls[1] and had prospered greatly since the opening of the Tay and Rideau Canals.

When his eyes had finally adjusted to the dim interior, Captain Leslie looked around the large store and admired the neatly arranged displays. Hardware, dry goods, medicinal drugs

---

[1] Carleton Place.

and fancy wares of every description, designed to meet the needs and desires of every settler for miles around, had been imported from Montreal, New York, London and Glasgow. From lacy Barcelona handkerchiefs to five hundredweight kegs of nails, precious India tea to weavers' reeds, W. & J. Bell had it all. They accepted pearl and pot ash, butter and hides as payment in exchange, which they in turn sold to markets in Montreal. Credit was a mainstay of all their business interests, which extended beyond the store into forwarding and land and industry speculation. Any upset in the precarious economy could be the ruin of them, and many others.

As John was busy with a customer, Captain Leslie went back to the office to meet with "young" William. Although only thirty-one years of age, grief had imbedded itself deeply into his face, making him look years older.

"I'm sorry for the loss of Maria, William," began Leslie. "How does the babe?"

William smiled wanly. "Well enough, I suppose. My mother cares for her and her sister." He took a long drink from a glass sitting at his right hand. "Sit down, captain. May I pour you one too? It's a very nice, local whisky that we've only just begun to carry. I imagine that's why you're here—to discuss our liquor vending licence—so you might as well sample the wares." Without waiting for an answer, William filled another glass and topped his up at the same time.

"Ah . . . it's a bit early . . . oh, well. Don't mind if I do."

The two men sat quietly for a moment, one savouring the delicate smoky flavour of a fine malt whisky, the other swallowing with numbing steadiness. William reached for the bottle and held it over Leslie's glass.

"No, I'm fine, thanks," refused the captain.

"Not turning into a temperance man, like my father, are you Leslie? He's become quite boring on the issue lately."

"No, it's just that . . ."

"Only teasing." William drained the bottle into his own glass and then very carefully placed it in a stained basket beside his desk. "Instead, let me show you what John and I have just got in.

Sure to interest you. Bit of a risk, but we felt that we couldn't—excuse me," he hiccupped, "—afford not to."

With careful steps, William walked over to the office safe and painstakingly unlocked it with one of the keys he held on a ring at his waist. From it, he reverently withdrew two notes and handed them to Captain Leslie for his inspection. Printed on only one side on very thin paper, these notes for fifteen and thirty pence had been expertly engraved. However, it was not the fine artwork that had caught the banker's eye. Instead, it was the proclamation, which Leslie read out loud, "On demand for Value received we promise to pay the Bearer one shilling and three pence in current banks bills in Sums not less than Five Shillings Currency. W. & J. Bell, Upper Canada."

Captain Leslie paused for a moment.

"But that's you!"

William just grinned as he toasted Leslie for his astute observation.

"Don't you think this calls for a celebration? Here, have some real *usquebaugh* to toast John's and my elevation to the ranks of the Rothchilds!"

"I think I'm more likely to raise a glass to your madness," countered Leslie. "Who printed these for you? How many did you get? How can you afford it?"

"Adolphus Bourne in Montreal. Four thousand of the quarter-dollar, or fifteen-pence; two thousand of the half-dollar, or thirty-pence notes. How could we afford not to?" ticked off William.

"Actually, John and I were a bit worried earlier this month when we realized how much it was going to cost just to get the notes printed, let alone finance their value. We didn't even think we had enough coin to pay the postage from Montreal so we asked Bourne to send the second shipment by stage with the Ottawa and Rideau Forwarding Company. He just put the notes in a box with wrapping paper and packed them off!" Tears of laughter streamed down William's face as he watched Leslie's slacken with incredulity over the tale he was hearing. They could laugh about it now, but both he and John had passed many an anxious moment since they had made the decision to proceed with the crazy scheme a month ago. Indeed, they had almost called it off at the beginning of August.

"You could have been ruined," said an awed Leslie. "You could still be ruined! Are you and John both mad? What has your father to say about all this?"

Wiping his eyes, William suddenly became serious. "The only madman in all of this," he began, leaning towards the banker, "is Sir Francis Bond Head. You know as well as anyone, if not better, the perennial shortage of coin in this province. And since the Specie Circular was issued three months ago, the Americans have been draining south any coin that we have been able to accumulate. We wrote the lieutenant-governor demanding that he sign a House of Assembly authorization allowing the Bank of Upper Canada to also suspend specie payments, to try and stem the flow of gold and silver, but still he sits on his big, fat ass—and does nothing! I swear that Bond Head is the greatest curse on this province and has done more to alienate the affections of the people than all the radicals could do for half a century."

An ugly red flush began creeping up over William's collar, gradually staining his face with rage.

"And, what with the crop failures this year, the depression in Britain, the financial panic in the United States and the political shenanigans raging unchecked in both provinces, I'll bet my last shinplaster that there's a revolt before the year is out!"

The Bells' shinplasters were soon circulating freely throughout the local economy, accepted as secure as Upper Canada Bank bills, which they could exchange their Bell scrip for when they had accumulated a minimum of five shillings worth. Buoyed by their initial success, William and John ordered more from Adolphus Bourne, who had discovered a lucrative sideline to his other engraving products. Bourne was already designing and printing notes issued by William and Thomas Molson for the Molson Brewery Company in Montreal and subsequently secured similar contracts for several other merchants in both provinces. In Upper Canada alone, as many as twelve merchant houses followed the Bell brothers' lead and issued their own notes in various denominations during this financial crisis.

Captain Leslie marvelled at William and John's audacity and envied their early success. By the end of the year, shopkeepers and farmers, pedlars and industrialists made purchases, paid bills and indulged fancies with six-pence, seven-and-one-half-pence, twelve-pence, fifteen-pence and thirty-pence shinplasters, all endorsed and secured by the Bell family's impeccable reputation. Although sniffed at by the authorities, there was nothing that could be done to curb their use.

In time, the upheavals of 1837 righted themselves and Captain Leslie returned to his orderly life of farming, fishing and banking—in that order. For the next two years, he continued to see Bell scrip cross his counter, although once the banks restored specie payments in late 1839, public opinion finally turned against it.

"Sir," puffed McFarlane, as he endeavoured to blow life into arthritic fingers cramped by the November chill, "did you see the advertisement in this week's issue of the *Bathurst Courier*? Your colleagues. Perth merchants. Refusing to accept shinplasters. Blow to the Bells."

"Yes, yes, McFarlane, I agree. But necessary. Specie is in unrestricted circulation now," declaimed Captain Leslie as he stepped out the door with a fishing pole over his shoulder, "and steps must be taken to prevent the total debasement of currency in this province."

COMMERCIAL BANK, M. D.

THE Undersigned having been appointed to the Agency of the above Bank, at Perth, U. C. gives notice that he will be in attendance at his Office during the usual business hours.

Bank drafts on Lower Canada or on the Upper Province can be obtained by applying at the Agent's Office here. From the late loss of money passing through the Post Office such drafts may be desirable to those requiring to remit.

All notes to be forwarded to Kingston for approval, require to be sent in the day before the departure of the Post, or they will have to remain until the next Post day, those to go by the Monday morning Post to be sent in on Saturday.

ANTHONY LESLIE,
Agent.

Perth, February 5, 1835.

Advertisements for the Commercial Bank, M.D. *Bathurst Courier* 5 February 1835.

W. & J. Bell.

IN addition to their present stock are now receiving their FALL and WINTER SUPPLY OF BRITISH AND AMERICAN GOODS, imported by themselves, the whole comprising an assortment unequalled by any before offered for sale in this district, amongst which will be found every description of Cloths, Calicoes, Shawls, Merinoes, Flannels, Serges, Blankets, Moleskins, Linens, Sheetings, American and British Silks and Ribbons, Cotton yarns, Buck mits, Fur caps, &c. &c. A splendid assortment of Hardware and Cutlery, Tools, Iron, Nails, Steel, Glass, &c. &c. Swords & Pistols, belts, Silk Sashes, Militia Buttons, Silver Cord, &c. &c. Drugs and Medicines, Paints, Crockery, Stationary and Books—Fish, Salt, American & English Parlor Stoves, Three Rivers and American Cooking do, the whole of which will be sold at uncommonly low prices, and produce received in payment.

Perth 1st November 1839.

FURS, &c. The highest price paid for Furs and Bear Skins, by
W. & J. Bell.

Perth 1s November 1839.

Advertisement for W. & J. Bell, *Bathurst Courier*, 22 November 1839.

Bell Brothers' shinplasters. *Credit: Perth Museum*

A CALL TO ARMS

"PHYSICAL IMPOSSIBILITY OF A REVOLUTION IN CANADA," screamed the headline in the *Bathurst Courier*. "Wearied with the accounts of incipient revolution among the French inhabitants of Lower Canada, we are induced to glance a moment at the possibility of bringing about any successful insurrection in the province alluded to . . ."[1]

Dr George Hume Reade continued to scan the article reprinted from the *New York Albion*, his eyebrows rising and falling in concert with the writer's arguments. As colonel of the Third Leeds Militia Regiment, he had more than a passing interest in the growing unrest that rumbled across the provinces. Eighteen thirty-seven had been a difficult summer for everyone, as North America plunged into a depression. There was no money, few crops and curtailed trade with England, and he feared that as winter closed down upon them, some of the more radical malcontents would take advantage of people's fears and revolt, despite what the American writer thought.

Finishing the article, he glanced at the lumber prices and results from last week's fall fair, and grunted. Only one yoke of oxen and two milch cows sold at the October gathering, which had attracted more cattle than people; lumber prices were up slightly, but shaky. How could you muster up loyalty in a government, he mused, when you had trouble feeding your family?

---

[1] *Bathurst Courier*, 6 October 1837.

On November sixth, 1837, a mass meeting organized in Montreal by *les Patriotes* spontaneously erupted into a riot. Louis-Joseph Papineau, long-time Speaker of the House of Assembly in Lower Canada and agitator for political reform, had purposely not attended the meeting for fear that his presence would spark further violence in a movement that was becoming known for bloodshed. The government interpreted his trip to the country as an attempt to obtain more armed support for a *coup d'état*. They dispatched regiments to the known centres of *Patriote* feeling and the two sides clashed bloodily at St-Eustache, St-Charles and St-Denis. Nevertheless, being more organized and better armed, the government forces soon quashed the rabble-rousers, but not before Papineau and his lieutenants had fled to safety in the United States, their accidental rebellion reduced to a farce.

Meanwhile, Papineau's counterpart in Upper Canada, the firebrand William Lyon Mackenzie, seized the opportunity presented by the *Patriote* uprising and issued his own call to action. Alarm swept both provinces, spurring farmers and millers, farriers and masons to join their militia regiments to strike down the insurgents. They wanted reform, not revolution.

Colonel Reade looked out over the assembled crowd. Nearly 200 men had packed this first rally of the Third Leeds Militia at Pike Falls.[2] He hoped he'd get as many at the one tomorrow night at Jebb's Creek. Their excited jabberings buzzed and bumped each other, a stew of fact and rumour, hopes and expectations. Well, whether they were here for glory or the Queen's shilling, it was Reade's job to marshall this enthusiasm into an efficient fighting force that he would personally march into Lower Canada, in the name of Her newly-crowned Majesty, Queen Alexandrina Victoria.

The drums of war were a familiar sound to Colonel Reade, although as an apothecary in the army, he had never actually led a fighting force. However, he had been able to parlay his loyalty into a substantial land grant at the Perth Military Settlement where he soon established a successful business in medicinal drugs. Much to his dismay, however, he had been unable to monopolize their sale in the settlement, especially during the

---

[2] Port Elmsley

cholera epidemic of 1832, when the supply of quinine could barely keep up with the demand. His professional and social standings also secured him the appointments at one time or another of health inspector, coroner, Justice of the Peace and Clerk of the Peace.

This rebellion, however, was a new challenge—one that threatened his way of life, and all that he had worked for, in a way that Napoleon never had. He would not fail his sovereign now, nor would those under his command. It was time to begin.

Colonel Reade signalled one of his lieutenants to call the meeting to order. It took some time before the junior officers could subdue the excited crowd and Reade took the time to concentrate on his messages of loyalty and duty.

"The circumstances which have induced me to command your attendance this day are of a nature that will arouse the feelings of every one possessing a spark of loyalty and attachment to the government of our most gracious and excellent Queen and a reverence for the laws and sacred institutions of our country."

A few rustling sounds skirmished with the colonel's words as the men at the back pressed forward in an attempt to hear.

". . . The equitable administration of our laws is considered oppressive and a grievance, the sovereign power is held up to contempt, and, in fact, no pains are taken to conceal the revolutionary intentions of a disloyal faction and their desire for a separation from the parent state . . ."

Colonel Reade had now warmed to his theme. In his world, you were either patriotic or traitorous, honourable or dishonourable, for or against.

". . . and is there one amongst us that can forget the kindness and indulgence that has been bestowed upon us in these very Townships; look at your respective homes and what is presented to your sight—well-cultivated farms, comfortable dwellings, comparative affluence, taxes not worth naming, the blessing of Education for your children at a cheap and moderate rate, and the ministers of God, no matter of whatever Christian sect or denomination, fostered and supported. Is there one of you, but must idolize the Sovereign power that has conferred so many benefits, and is there one can now refuse his aid in supporting that power."

The aches and pains of back-breaking labour clearing thick bush from rock-riddled soil were eased by the colonel's words. No more did these men worry about how they would feed their families over the coming winter with the pickings from a lean harvest. They would fight to protect what was theirs.

"I now call upon you to step forward and volunteer your services for Lower Canada, there to maintain the character of a British soldier defending whatever may be entrusted to your fidelity."[3]

The room erupted with three cheers for the young queen, and before the night was done, 170 men had volunteered.

Everywhere, men were marching. Answering the call to protect hearth and home from the faithless faction who threatened their way of life, they drilled for hours on end with ancient muskets and handmade paper cartridges. Bite off the bullet. Pour the powder down the barrel, leaving a pinch for priming. Spit in the ball. Ramrod out, up and down the barrel. Remove the ramrod. Raise the musket. Pull back the cock. Prime the pan. Fire. Repeat the process. An experienced soldier could fire three shots a minute and, in the heat of battle, maybe four or five. His range? One hundred and seventy-five yards.

Bit by bit, aging veterans remembered the formations of their youth, while those who had not yet been born when the stench of sulphur cloaked battlefields from Badajoz to Michilimackinac despaired of grasping even a hint of the skills that it took a British regular soldier three years to master. One day in June was not enough.

Left! Left! Left, right, left!

The Perth Artillery Company, to a man, marched down the streets of Perth in time to the thrill of fife and drums. They had been ordered to Brockville where they would join other regiments also going to the lower province.

Left! Left! Left, right, left!

A clutch of keening Irishwomen tore their hair and wailed their loss as they watched their sons march by. When would war stop demanding this sacrifice? Young girls fluttered tokens of

[3] Excerpts from Colonel George Hume Reade's Speech to the Third Leeds Militia, 23 November 1837, as printed in the *Bathurst Courier*, 1 December 1837.

their devotion at the handsome soldiers who, just a few days before, had been nondescript farm boys. Would they come back to keep their promises?

Left! Left! Left, right, left!

The Reverend William Bell closed First Presbyterian's heavy door against the martial rhythms that thundered through the town. Today was a day of fasting and humiliation. He began his service with a prayer for peace.

It was the seventh day of December, eighteen hundred and thirty-seven.

Within days, they heard word of Mackenzie's march down Yonge Street on December fifth, and the ragged skirmish across stump fences north of Toronto. The stories of the uprising fed voraciously on speculation and fear until they assumed monstrous proportions. The rebels had taken and sacked Toronto. They had plundered the banks. They had hanged the government. However, the one truth amongst all this rumour was that the hot-tempered rebel leader had escaped capture, sending the entire countryside into a panic as everyone rummaged through haystacks looking for dissidents.

They thought they had found three outside Perth on the Scotch Line, so they had them arrested and brought into town on a charge of treason. Fortunately, cool heads prevailed and found the accusations to be groundless.

William Morris called the meeting to order. The courthouse was stifling, despite the chill mid-December day, from the more than 100 men who had heeded the magistrates' call to arms. As both commanding colonel of the Second Lanark Militia and member of the Legislative Council, everyone acknowledged him as the most qualified to lead them in this time of crisis.

"Our purpose here today," he began, "is to form a volunteer corps to do duty in town and mount a nightly guard until order is restored." He then proceeded to inform them of the rebellion in Upper Canada and of the one-thousand-pound reward for the apprehension and deliverance to justice of the rebel, William Lyon Mackenzie.

"I know that the people of Perth and Bathurst are loyal to the crown and state and that we have no real fear for alarm, but this is not the time to abandon our government or our defences. We will be prepared for any emergency, against any miscreant who might take advantage of the situation. For the evil disposed in other parts of the country may take it into their heads to send emissaries to this peaceful population and attack during the night, when all are fast asleep."

Visions of marauding thugs assaulted the throng, churning their fears and enthusiasm into a military fever. William Morris' oratory had done the job again. Nearly every man there eagerly joined Perth's newly formed Volunteer Corps.

By December fifteenth, the Perth Artillery Company under the command of Captain Henry Graham had returned to Perth, the escalation of events in Upper Canada demanding their presence at home. Captain Fraser, with the assistance of Lieutenant Haggart and Ensign John Bell, had instituted regular drills of the Volunteer Corps and the nightly guard, while Colonels McMillan and Morris, of the First and Second Lanark Militias respectively, had ordered weekly drills for their regiments until further notice. The Perth Artillery Company drilled daily.

The *Bathurst Courier* challenged, "LET THEM COME IF THEY DARE!"[4] Perth was ready.

Colonel Reade continued his recruitment drive for the Third Leeds, holding meetings throughout Elmsley Township. Today, the call had exceeded all his expectations. Five hundred and eighty men had gathered at the Ferry, oblivious to the December cold as he read out the Militia General Order. Many had signed up already at either Pike Falls or Jebb's Creek, but there were a great many new faces here who were keen to make their mark. He had sent his new captain, John Bell, to Smiths Falls to recruit even more men, as he expected his regiment to be called up to Toronto any day.

---

[4] *Bathurst Courier*, 15 December 1837.

Reade dreamed of military glory as he reviewed his troops going through their drill exercises. A shimmering vision of gold braid clouded his view of the farmers' clumsy attempts to handle weapons, which ranged from umbrellas to Brown Besses. The three cheers to queen, constitution and Sir Francis Bond Head deafened him to the shouts and curses as lumbermen crashed into each other, unable to follow their lieutenants' barked orders.

And later that night at a special dinner, he basked in the reflected glory of his officers as they toasted their loyalty to Lieutenant-Governor Sir Francis Bond Head, Lieutenant-General Sir John Colborne, and their commanding officer, Colonel George Hume Reade.

Christmas came and went, and still the rebel leaders remained at large, seeking refuge and support in the United States. In January, the Third Leeds Militia and the Perth Artillery Company were ordered to Kingston—the latter the first Canadian garrison at the newly built Fort Henry—to help defend the border against any raids from Americans who desired to throw off the mantle of British rule from the whole of the North American continent. For their loyalty, they were promised—and eventually received—one shilling a day, one overcoat, one pair of trousers, one cap, one pair of shoes and one pair of mitts. Clothed and fed, many of Perth's sons spent a relatively comfortable winter keeping watch for the invaders who never came.

On Sunday the twenty-fifth of May, 1838, the Perth Artillery Company returned home from Fort Henry minus one comrade who had died under unfortunate circumstances. They had distinguished themselves in Kingston and, before embarking on the steamship *Cataraqui*, which carried them up the Rideau to the Perth Landing, the band of the 83rd Regiment expressed the appreciation of the entire city of Kingston with a stirring send-off.

So, while men like Colonel Reade never found their military glory in downing the failed uprising, Reverend Bell summed it up best:

Never was a rebellion more disastrous to its authors, or attended with less bloodshed to the friends of government.[5]

May it ever be so.

---

[5] Rev. Wm. Bell Diaries, December 1837.

Tête de Pont (Fort Frontenac) Barracks, Kingston. Sketch by J.P. Cockburn, 1830.
Credit: Public Archives of Canada

A MATTER OF HONOUR

The dampness misted over him like a shroud. Small rivulets of water trickled down his face, clouding his vision. Or was it sweat? He could not get his hands dry. He kept wiping them against his trousers, but the clamminess wouldn't go away. And cold! His hands were so cold, cold as gunmetal.

One, two, three, four. His heart was beating so loudly, he was forced to count its steady rhythm. Five, six, seven, eight. It suddenly became very important to be able to do this. Nine, ten.

The Almighty suddenly roared His outrage, sending blood to thunder in his ears and drown out all conscious thought. Lightning exploded in the sky, and life screamed apocalypse.

Where were they? John Wilson, an earnest, hard-working and pious young man, could not find those contracts. Deeds, wills, summonses, court documents—all these he could find in plenty on his overworked desk, but nowhere could he locate any contract dealing with the Tay Navigation Company. As a student-at-law, it was Wilson's responsibility to keep all the paperwork in order. William Morris, one of the principals of the Tay Navigation Company, was due to arrive any minute to collect the completed documents. Mr Morris was off to Montreal in the morning and these contracts would, he hoped, convince the Montreal investors to provide the necessary funds that would allow the completion of the vital transportation link between Perth and the Rideau Canal.

He could hear footsteps coming down the hall. Where were those contracts? He'd been working on them yesterday, and then Colonel Matheson had arrived and insisted that Wilson attend to his business immediately. Maybe they got mixed in with Matheson's file?

The steady, determined steps made unwavering progress down the long, central hallway. SQUEAK. That board was five steps from the door and its signal had alerted Wilson to attention on many an occasion, when a lack of sleep had caused him to doze off in the middle of copying documents. The steps stopped at the doorway. Eureka! Wilson espied the missing contracts and, with an exclamation of triumph, seized them from beneath an extremely weighty tome on the law of evidence. A small avalanche of precedents went crashing to the floor.

"Oh, I'm sorry," a soft, feminine voice apologized. "Did I startle you?"

Wilson looked up in confusion, feeling rather silly waving the white parchment in the air like some Roman orator amongst the ruins of Pompeii.

"I've just come to inform you, Mr Wilson," she calmly announced, "that Mr Morris' man is here to collect his documents. I was passing through the hallway when he arrived and said that I would make you aware of his arrival."

"Yes, yes of course, Miss Hughes. Thank you, Miss Hughes. I have them right here and I will take them to him directly."

Why did he always manage to behave like a flaming idiot when the governess was around? She was only an employee of the Boultons, like himself, but she always seemed to convey the impression that she was superior to him.

And, oh, he was in love with her! Desperately, hopelessly and impossibly in love with her. Late at night, after he had finished his studies and when only a small stub of candle sputtered in its saucer, he would inadequately pour out on paper his thoughts, dreams and desires for the fair Elizabeth.

What can it be that makes me sad?
*   I surely can't be turning mad*
And yet, indeed, 'tis very plain
*   I am in ____; let me think again.*
It cannot be, for love is bliss,
*   Not a heart-rending thing like this —*
'Tis true there's one bewitching being,
*   And one whom I can scarce help seeing,*
Who makes me every time we meet
*   Fain to say something wondrous sweet'.*
But how it is you won't believe,
*   My memory is a perfect sieve,*
And pretty speeches fly; you laugh!
*   Just as the whirlwind blows the chaff;*
And then I feel so quite put out,
*   'Tis no great wonder that I pout.*
Besides, you know, 'Tis wracking pain
*   "To live and not be loved again."*
And if the matter should thus be
*   What shall I do? Now come, let's see*
Why I'll turn poet and I'll sing
*   That loving is a desperate thing.*
But this won't do, for sure enough,
*   They'll say 'Tis canting, childish stuff.*
Well then, I'll try, well what d'ye say.
*   I'll mourn and fret ofr one short day*
And bear't after, as I may.

Wilson looked down at his hands, which were crushing the contracts. Large, rough and red, they were still a labourer's hands, even though it had been several years since he had left his father's stony homestead in the hills of North Sherbrooke. He worked with his mind now, teaching school in the early morning, articling with James Boulton during the day and studying, with the Reverend Bell's help, at night. But, no matter what he did, he could not shake the muck from his boots.

And Joanna. He'd pledged her his troth, he guiltily remembered, but it was hard to recall her affections when he was faced with Elizabeth.

Suddenly, he recalled himself. He quickly smoothed the papers, straightened his coat and collar, and went to meet the messenger, the very pattern card of a conscientious young lawyer.

Robert Lyon was a happy man. It was a beautiful spring day, he had concluded his business satisfactorily, and it was now time to wash away all the cares of the world with a tankard of best ale. Bytown had no shortage of taverns in which to pass his time and he had plenty of coin in his pocket to ensure that his sojourn would be a pleasant one.

Tall, handsome and with a genial disposition, Lyon made quite a contrast to the flotsam and jetsam that usually walked the streets of Bytown. Youngest child of George Lyon, sometime bailie, or mayor, of Inverurie, Aberdeenshire, he had followed his eldest brother, also George, to a new life in Upper Canada.

George the younger was a decorated officer of the War of 1812 and had accepted the government's generous offer of 800 acres near Richmond as a reward for his loyal services. He had settled himself comfortably and was fulfilling his responsibilities to the growing colony by taking on the positions of pension agent and Justice of the Peace. He had also ensured that his young brother would be prepared to assume his responsibilities and take his proper place in society by securing an articling position with his brother-in-law, Thomas Radenhurst, who lived in the nearby military settlement of Perth.

Bytown was the headquarters for the construction of the newly completed Rideau Canal. A military project designed to provide an inland supply route between Montreal and Kingston, secure against any future American invasion, it promised to be a real commercial boon to the settlements it passed through.

Many of the starving Irish who had been disgorged from the ships at Montreal had flocked to the dozens of building sites scattered throughout the uncut wilderness in search of a day's work. Unskilled, they worked as navvies—mules for the Scottish stone masons and English sappers and miners. Some tried to increase their wages by taking on the blasting jobs; many, in consequence, were then blown to pieces or left maimed to beg on the streets. And all because they hungered after a decent meal.

Those who survived intact often ended up in Bytown and turned their hopes to the Ottawa Valley lumber trade. The Irish saw that there was better money to be made on the rafts and in the bush and started fighting their way into the Canadian-controlled lumber camps. It was a rare day indeed when the two factions did not explode in a snarl of legs and arms on the streets of Bytown.

Lyon seemed impervious to all these little power struggles for hope and life as he navigated his way through the rest of the muck that oozed into Bytown's streets. Life had always been easy for him and, despite the Reformist politics of his employer, he expected all that was due to him through the circumstances of his birth. Raised to be a gentleman, he had been instructed in all the gentlemanly arts and imbued with the deep sense of honour that went with that title.

Ignoring the blandishments of the whores who lolled outside the taverns, Lyon entered the dark door of a Lowertown alehouse. It took him a few seconds to adjust his eyes to the smoky gloom. A couple of drunken soldiers, singing the virtues of some accommodating lass, jostled him out of the way. He carefully picked his way through the crowd and secured a stool lately vacated by a lout who didn't like it that a mere serving wench had spurned his advances. Thwarted in his efforts to chase after the girl by the crush of other drinkers, he reeled drunkenly back to his seat.

"Aye! What say you?" he belched. "That seat belongs to Daniel Butler. When I got off that coffin ship at Montreal, they gave me a location ticket for just that spot and ol' Jonathan here is going to give me m'deed just as soon as I drink him dry."

The tavern, obviously well acquainted with the rummy Daniel, roared with laughter as they weighed the odds between the fancy outsider and their local bruiser. Daniel was a good-sized man and had survived his fair share of fights amongst the brawling ethnic factions of Bytown and Montreal. But years of enjoying the Yankee's ale had begun to take their toll on Daniel. Greasy black hair straggled across bloodshot eyes and his broken nose bent down to his few remaining jagged teeth. His shoulders slumped into a flaccid chest and a massive belly did its best to hide his stump-like legs from view.

Daniel lurched towards Lyon with his right arm extended like a medieval battering ram. Lyon tilted back on his stool and watched Daniel go crashing down the table. Everyone in the tavern roared with laughter, and Daniel's supporters urged him to get up and go again. Others accused the colonial nob of having more brass than balls and taunted him to fight like a man.

Lyon decided to humour them and, when Daniel charged him again, fired a strong right. "Ooof," gasped a surprised Daniel as Lyon's fist deflated the drunk's soft belly. It was like punching down bread dough, thought Lyon, as he watched his opponent fall, clutching his gut. Daniel, for a moment stunned and supine on the littered dirt floor, rolled over and retched.

The room froze in a sudden hush, and then conversations started in a dozen different directions as the crowd realized that the young gentleman was very muscular beneath his tailored clothes. The Yankee tavern keeper hurried over with a tankard of ale and placed it on the table before Lyon. When Lyon reached for his purse, the shabby host forestalled him with a muttered, "Compliments of the house."

"Always the peacock, aren't you Lyon?"

Lyon, gratefully slaking his thirst with the Yankee's ale, glanced up over the rim of his tankard. Carefully, almost delicately, as if the battered pewter tankard were made of the finest Irish crystal, Lyon put his ale down on the stained trestle-table. A cold hauteur settled itself across his features, as, peering down his long nose, his eyes slowly rose up the figure of the slight man before him 'til it seemed that it was he who was standing above his challenger, and not the other way round. Lyon's steady gaze took in the cracked, mud-covered boots, the faded trousers and the ill-fitting coat that had been turned at the cuffs. He paused briefly at the limp cravat before meeting the challenging glare of John Wilson.

Although roughly the same age, as well as being fellow students-at-law in the town of Perth, they could not have been more unlike. While Lyon possessed and exhibited all the advantages of his birth and position, Wilson had only his amazing capacity for work and overwhelming ambition with which to attract attention. They also worked for sworn enemies.

"Why, did you want in on the action?" drawled Lyon. "If I had even known you were here, my dear Wilson, I would have alerted Mr Butler to the fact and let you take the fall."

"What really brings you to Bytown, Lyon?" demanded Wilson. "Are you `executing' more orders for that bastard you call employer, or did you just feel," he sneered with a sweep of his hand, "a need to associate with some of your own kind?"

"For shame, Wilson," Lyon responded with a flick of his fingers at an imaginary speck of dust on his immaculate coat sleeve. "I just came into this fine establishment for a pint of ale and a bit of feminine company." He looked over Wilson's shoulder and smiled invitingly at the wench who had been trying to catch his eye for the last ten minutes.

Lyon lazily returned his gaze to Wilson and sighed.

"Perth is decidedly lonely these days, now that a delightful young lady has abandoned my companionship for that of another, more `Gallic' gentleman. But, of course, you must be feeling the same pain as I, since you too have hoped for a *tendre* from that direction."

"Why, you . . ." Wilson growled. He lunged across the table, but Lyon had nimbly jumped up away from his grasp, in time to grab the lass who had answered his invitation.

"In fact, Wilson, LeLièvre and I have frequently had the very delightful pleasure of a turn in the garden with those alluring ladies of the Boulton household. The bench under the lilac trees is a charming place for a comfortable coze."

Laughing, Lyon bussed the girl loudly and yelled out to the landlord for directions to a room. With the press of people around him, Wilson could not catch Lyon, as the latter retreated to enjoy amorous pursuits.

The day's mail stood between the teapot and the sugar bowl. A plate of bread and butter sat daintily to the left and a fresh bouquet of June roses spilled out of a china vase in the middle of the table. Mrs Ackland flicked through the mail, selecting those letters addressed to her and Miss Hughes, before passing the remainder to her husband.

"Nothing terribly exciting today. Mostly correspondence relating to the school, Gideon. Although there is a note from that Mr LeLièvre for you, Elizabeth. I thought that Gideon had advised you of the inappropriateness of that liaison and you had broken off all contact with him."

"La, ma'am," replied Miss Hughes, "Perth society is so small, it is difficult to avoid anyone altogether, no matter how much you might want to discourage an acquaintance. But you must admit, he is so very amusing and exciting, in a slightly dangerous sort of way."

"Exactly my point, Elizabeth," said Gideon Ackland, master of a select school for young ladies, as he began to open his mail. The Acklands provided Elizabeth with both employment and home since the sudden death of her father from cholera shortly after the family's arrival in the Canadas the previous year. "You need someone with a good head on his shoulders and his feet firmly on the ground. Someone like John Wilson. He is a fine, upstanding young man with a great future ahead of him, with the trust of his superiors. I know that he holds you in high regard and . . . speak of the—here's a letter from him in Bytown. See, he holds Boulton's trust to represent him in his offices down there."

"Oh, I know he has a *tendre* for me—he wrote me a valentine—but he's just a poor school teacher pretending to be a lawyer. Besides," she sniffed, "I heard that he has an understanding with some farm girl—Joanne, Joanna—from wherever it is he's from."

Elizabeth resumed eating her breakfast but was quickly distracted by the grave look descending over Mr Ackland's face.

"Whatever is the matter. Surely, it's not bad news?"

"It is the worst kind of news, Elizabeth." Gideon Ackland's voice was cold with foreboding. "If this is true, you have been both indiscreet and extremely foolhardy."

"Whatever can you mean?" asked Elizabeth.

"I mean that you and Caroline Thom, while under the escort of Mr Lyon, have been meeting that `well-dressed, idle nobody'—as your brother so aptly puts it—Henri LeLièvre. And, to make matters worse, you have allowed Lyon to sit alongside you with his arms about you in," and here he referred to the letter, "in `a position which no woman of spirit would permit'!"

"But that is false, Mr Ackland," contradicted a shocked Miss Hughes. "True, Caroline and I have enjoyed the company of Mr Lyon. But never, ever has either one of us behaved in any way that would reflect badly on the school or ourselves. Mr Wilson has been terribly misinformed by some malicious gossip-monger and seeks only to hurt me with these lies."

Elizabeth was crying by the time she had finished her defence. And, all thoughts of breakfast gone, she ran from the room.

"I am sure, sir, that you understand the gravity of these allegations and, as they involve your sister-in-law, Miss Thom, I was confident that you would wish to be made aware of them."

"You are quite right, Gideon," replied James Boulton gravely. Although only thirty-two, James Boulton had already achieved considerable success in life. A lawyer, and member of one of Upper Canada's most powerful families, he had erected the first brick house in Perth shortly after his arrival a decade ago. The Summit House was not only one of the largest houses in the province, it also commanded the most influential site in this capital of the District of Bathurst. Next to the Church of England, Church of Rome and the courthouse, the two-storey, red-brick, Georgian mansion sat atop the hill overlooking the Tay River, which ran through the middle of the town. A hot-tempered man, with a strong sense of class and honour, he had engaged in more than one physical confrontation with the two other members of Perth's legal fraternity: "upstart" Daniel McMartin and "reformer" Thomas Radenhurst. He possessed an especial hatred for the latter, whom he had met on a field of honour in New York state. In fact, this hatred almost amounted to a family feud dating back more than fifteen years. In 1817, his brother John had met Radenhurst's brother-in-law, Samuel Ridout, in York, with pistols.

"We both know John Wilson to be an honest, God-fearing man with no reason to lie. And Robert Lyon . . ." Boulton sneered, "anyone who is both related to and employed by that whoreson

Radenhurst cannot be expected to respect even a scullery maid, let alone ladies. Caroline!"

Boulton had thrown open the door of his library and bellowed into the house. Very quickly, his sister-in-law appeared in answer to his belligerent summons.

"I have just received a very distressing communication, pertaining to the actions of you, Caroline, and Miss Hughes. And if there is even a shred of truth to these allegations, Caroline, I will have to insist that Harriet dispense with the services of Miss Hughes. I will not have a woman of such low moral character instructing my children."

"Why James," fluttered Caroline, "I cannot possibly think what you mean." Caroline Thom was very pretty and very feminine and very used to placating bombastic men. Her father, Dr Alexander Thom, an army surgeon more interested in commerce than medicine, was not known for his calm bedside manner.

"I mean this!" He thrust John Wilson's letter into her face.

Caroline quickly scanned the contents of the letter. Her mind, working just as fast, frantically sought a way out of this situation. There was a grain of truth in the story, but considering the original source and the state of relations all round, she was sure that she could salvage her reputation.

"Really, James," Caroline casually tossed the letter onto her brother-in-law's desk. "How can you give any credence to a story that was manufactured by Robert Lyon? I will most certainly give him the cut direct the next time I encounter him, and I will definitely advise Elizabeth to do the same."

And with that, Caroline picked up her skirts, turned and exited the room.

Lyon was marching very determinedly up the hill to the courthouse, his long strides making short work of the steep incline. Ever since his return home yesterday, people had been giving him the cold shoulder. Caroline Thom had refused even to acknowledge his presence, which was in complete contrast to her behaviour not long ago in her brother-in-law's garden, he remembered with a smile.

As he approached the courthouse, he saw his friend Henri LeLièvre. A handsome man who exuded an air of continental sophistication not often found in Upper Canada, LeLièvre was the younger son of a French naval officer who had changed sides during the Napoleonic Wars. He had recently returned to Perth where his father at one time had held a grant of 800 acres in payment for services rendered to the Royal Navy. LeLièvre was always available to escort a lady while she made her calls or make up the numbers at a dinner party.

"Well, well, my young friend," LeLièvre greeted Lyon. "What is this I hear of you telling tales out of school?"

"I wish that someone would tell me what tales are going 'round about me."

"Come now, Lyon. What can you expect when you besmirch a lady's good name? Especially a lady who enjoys the protection of Messieurs Ackland and Boulton. 'Tis odd, though, I do not ever recall her being so receptive to my advances, to my great regret."

Lyon's annoyance at this illumination quickly turned to anger. Coming up the courthouse walk was Gideon Ackland who, in addition to teaching, also studied law.

"Ackland!" Lyon barked. "What vile lies have you been spreading about me?"

"I've done no such thing, Lyon," responded Ackland coolly, "and I would appreciate it if you would not make a spectacle of yourself in a public place.

"Anything that I might have mentioned, in reference to your actions, is no surprise to those of us who know your true character. The only difference now is that I have written proof."

"I demand that you tell me the name of this libeller."

"What, you have so many enemies that you need me to sort them out for you?" demanded Ackland.

Robert Lyon looked as if he was about to commit murder right there on the courthouse steps. Henri LeLièvre walked nonchalantly up to the two men.

"By the way, my friend," he asked as if seeking direction, "where is Wilson these days?"

"Robert, we have walked up and down every single street in Perth, and I tell you, if Wilson has indeed returned from Bytown, he is making himself scarce." The day was hot and the streets dusty, but Lyon turned a deaf ear to Adam Muir's complaints, and the latter almost had to run to keep up to his determined friend. Lyon had come by earlier that day and had insisted that Muir accompany him on his search for Wilson. He wanted Muir to be a witness to any confrontation.

"All I want to do, Adam, is ask that bastard to confirm the allegations he made against me, and then, when he says yes, knock him from here to kingdom come. You will be a witness to Wilson's admission of guilt."

They rounded a corner but, because of the high fence, could not see anyone coming the other way. Wilson and Lyon collided.

"I knew if I looked under enough rocks, I'd find you." Lyon had reacted quickly to the encounter and had slammed the smaller man hard against the fence.

"Tell me, did you write that letter to Ackland?"

"So what if I did?" Wilson gasped defensively. "Miss Hughes is too good for someone like you."

"I think it's time that you and I sorted a few things out, farm boy," Lyon sneered, his handsome face marred by hatred and rage. "As a student-at-law, you should know that society exists because of order. And the natural order of things dictates that you are scum, always have been and always will be. Now, as I recall, scum live in mud, but somehow or other, you've managed to ooze out."

Lyon's breath on Wilson's face was hot and foul with liquor. Wilson tried desperately to struggle free so that he could take a swing at the younger man, but Lyon was just too strong for him. He tried to trip him but was halted by a swift knee to the groin.

"Hey, easy there Robert," Muir interjected. "You've roughed him up and I don't think he'll be giving you any more trouble. He'll know now to keep his place and not go sticking his nose into the affairs of his betters."

"I'm not finished instructing him yet, Adam," Lyon grunted. "He's a damned lying scoundrel, and I think he's in need of some private lessons."

Lyon grabbed Wilson under the arms and dragged him, struggling, behind the fence. Muir winced at the sound of frequent blows and long moans of pain.

❧

"Good Lord, John, what in God's name has happened to you?"

John Wilson staggered into Gideon Ackland's sitting room and fell into the chair closest to the door. His clothes were torn and muddy, and his nose was bleeding, the blood mixed with that from the cuts on his face. One eye, a glorious kaleidoscope of colour, was rapidly swelling shut.

"Ran into Lyon," he grimaced.

"More like a brick wall!" exclaimed another law student, Simon Fraser Robertson, who was also there.

"Not quite, just a wooden fence."

"This is inexcusable, John. I'm going over there right now and . . ."

"Don't bother, Gideon. He refuses to speak to you. He knows I wrote you the letter and he's not interested in any explanations. I insulted him, so he was obliged to obtain satisfaction." Wilson tested his jaw and winced. "God, he and his kind make me ill. By the mere accident of birth, he thinks he can lord it over me; well, I'm not standing for it. Not any more. Now I'm not satisfied, not by a long shot."

"John, what are you babbling about?"

"Honour! Gideon. Surely as a gentleman, and an aspiring member to the bar, you understand honour? And how it must be upheld, at all costs, against the barbarous influences of the lower classes?" Wilson adopted a high-pitched, nasal tone.

"Yes, uh, no, John . . ."

"Yes, Gideon. The only way I am ever going to be respected in this town is if I meet Lyon on his terms. Simon," he turned to the other man, "I want you to take Mr Lyon a message."

Simon paled.

"Tell him to name his seconds."

The sweet scent of lilacs was carried into the house on the arms of a soft June breeze. Outside, children were playing in the warm sunshine and the Ackland maid was hanging up the wet laundry. Gideon, stunned by John's order to Simon, finally breathed.

"John, I must vigorously protest this course of action."

"I too, John," agreed Simon Fraser Robertson.

"Before you send Simon anywhere," continued Gideon quickly, "I must insist that you speak with Mr Boulton. You are not thinking clearly. In fact, by the look of those wounds, I wouldn't be at all surprised if you were concussed. Yes, that's it. You're concussed," he laughed shakily. "You have to be. You disapprove of duelling so you would have to have a very serious head injury if you would even think about challenging a sportsman like Lyon to a duel."

"I'll ask Boulton to come here," volunteered Simon. "I'm sure, among us, we can devise some other solution. I know Robert well. He was just blowing off a little steam and I'm sure he's forgotten all about it by now. A simple apology all 'round, and then it's drinks on me." Simon's attempts at cheer were having no effect at dispelling the feeling of dread that permeated the otherwise comfortable room.

"Yes, Simon," agreed Gideon desperately. "Go get Boulton. I believe he's at the courthouse. Hurry."

Simon left the room, and they soon heard his footsteps running anxiously down the street. The two friends sat silently basking in the rays of the late afternoon sunshine. Gideon rose and went to the kitchen for a towel and some water. Gently, he cleaned the crusted blood from his friend's face.

"You and I have been intimates a long time John," Gideon remarked calmly.

Wilson grunted noncommittally.

"I've watched you work eighteen hours a day—teaching school in the morning, studying in the evening and articling for Boulton during the day. You assist Reverend Bell with his sabbath school and you oppose violence of any kind. I also know that you manage to send some of your earnings home to your mother."

Wilson grunted again. Gideon sighed and tried another tack.

"You have come so far in such a short time for the son of a poor Paisley weaver. And I know that you have a brilliant future ahead of you. Why do you want to risk it all by standing on some blasted `field of honour' and getting blasted to smithereens? Good God, man, you're only twenty-three years old!"

Voices and boots clumped together in the hallway. Gideon and John looked up to see Simon and James Boulton enter the room.

"Well, John, you're a fine sight," remarked Boulton. "I thought farm boys learned to fight before they learned to walk?"

Wilson, touching the towel to his swollen lip, made no response.

Boulton frowned as he slowly walked around the small room. He came to a stop near the fireplace and stared fixedly at a sampler hanging above Wilson's left shoulder.

"The decision to challenge another to a duel," he began unemotionally, as if he were delivering a lecture on some precise point of law, "is a serious one and should only be undertaken if all other courses of reconciliation are deemed to be hopeless. And once issued, it is difficult to retract that challenge, if not impossible, and still retain your honour. I know," and here he looked, momentarily, straight into Wilson's eyes. "And because I know, I certainly do not feel that I can advise you one way or the other on what your ultimate course of action should be. This is your decision, John, and yours alone."

Boulton resumed his professorial perambulating. Wilson, eyes closed and apparently lost in pain, suddenly sat up and turned to Robertson.

"Simon, I want you to offer Lyon two options," he pronounced quietly. "Lyon can either make me a formal apology or he can meet me. His choice."

❧

BAM! BAM! BAM!

What was that infernal noise?

BAM! BAM! BAM!

Ohh, he remembered. Raw whisky. He'd been over at Henry Glass' last night—the bootlegger—and they'd been sampling the latest batch. It had tasted pretty smooth at the time, but as his tongue made its rough journey around the inside of his mouth, he was beginning to have second thoughts. He was in no shape to forward his critique right now, but he would be sure to do so once he woke up. Maybe next week, after his head stopped pounding.

BAM! BAM! BAM!

That wasn't his head. It was the door. Why would the door be pounding? It was an inanimate object. Inanimate objects made no noise. He would have to speak to the door and remind it that it was incapable of making any noise as prescribed by the laws of nature.

"Adam, you old sot!"

It was Robert, Adam Muir groggily acknowledged. Good. He would tell Robert to tell the door about its proper place, and he could go back to bed. Robert was good at things like that.

"It's about time you appeared," Lyon boomed. "I've been pounding on that infernal door for ten minutes."

"Yes, Robert," Adam replied weakly, clutching his head. "I want to talk to you about the door's pounding, it's not right . . ."

"You're damn right, it's not right, and you and I, my pickled friend," he wrinkled his nose as he passed Adam, "are going to meet Wilson and Robertson and show them so."

"Going, Robert? Where are we going?"

"To a duel, Adam."

Instantly, Adam Muir was as sober as if he'd been doused with a pail full of ice water.

"You're mad Robert. No," he turned to peer at the small clock just then chiming from the mantlepiece, "you're sleepwalking. It's only six o'clock!"

"No, I am wide awake and very sane." Lyon walked into the room, sat down in the one chair the room boasted and put his feet up on the cold grate as casually as if he'd come to make a social call. "Wilson has challenged me to a duel, and I've accepted. I want you to be my second."

"You are mad."

"Oh, I was last night when I agreed to sign that nonsensical apology and Wilson agreed to acknowledge that that `poison-pen' letter had been misunderstood, but I soon saw reason.

"So, I need a second and I immediately thought of you. Only good manners, I thought, as you were witness to the first challenge."

The clock ticked steadily in the quiet room. The morning sun was quickly chasing away the few remaining shadows of the night, but Adam could not shake the feeling of dark foreboding.

"No, Robert, I won't."

"There's nothing to be afraid of, Adam." Robert looked up at his friend who was standing shell-shocked in his stained nightshirt. "You know I'm a crack shot and I don't think Wilson could even hit the broad side of a byre. We'll trot out across the town limits, so as not to embarrass the sheriff, pace off and fire. I may graze him, just as a warning, and he'll scare a few chipmunks. We'll all be home in time for dinner. Just like the duel between Thom and McMillan back in January."

"No Robert, I won't."

"Look, I've obviously got you up from your bed. You wash, shave, have some breakfast—that will make you feel better—burn that shirt, and I'll be back in a few hours to confirm the arrangements."

Adam stood for a long time, after Lyon had left, in the middle of the room, staring at the clock. Somehow, he felt if he stared at it long enough, it would start going backwards, and he would, blessedly, have a hangover again.

"No Robert," Adam insisted, "I've shaved, washed, had my breakfast and sent my nightshirt to the washerwoman's, but I have not changed my mind. I thank you for the 'honour' of your invitation, but I will not be your second and I urgently advise you to sign that apology."

It was now after nine o'clock and Robert Lyon had returned with Henri LeLièvre to find that Adam Muir was still adamant in his refusal. He had tried bullying, cajoling and reasoning, but to no avail. Adam would not do it.

"I need a second," Robert insisted. "Everything is arranged for six o'clock this evening, on the banks of the Tay just beyond the town limits, on Colonel Powell's farm. Dr Hamilton has agreed to officiate, and slap some sticking plaster if need be, but I must have a second."

No one said anything, the only sound in the small room being the ticking of the mantle clock.

"Well, the solution is very simple," offered LeLièvre casually. "If Muir refuses to be your second, then I must take up the gauntlet, so to speak. Wilson has insulted your good name and, therefore, must not be allowed to go unanswered."

"You, LeLièvre?" both Robert and Adam looked at the French dandy.

"Well, why not?" Robert answered the question with dawning delight. He strode up to his second, shook his hand vigorously and, with his other hand, thumped him on the shoulder. "We'll make a glorious display on the field."

Thursday, the thirteenth day of June, 1833 was very still and muggy. Throughout the day, people commented to each other that there was a storm brewing and that it would probably break before nightfall. They also shook their heads over the fight between Lyon and Wilson. Young men, they concluded, always had to settle their disputes with fists. They'd grow out of it.

Adam Muir had spent most of the day pacing in his small quarters. More than once, he started out the door, stopped and then went back inside. He had conflicting feelings over his decision not to stand as Lyon's second. On one hand, as a gentleman, he was obliged to uphold a friend's honour. On the other hand, duelling with pistols was a madman's solution. The clouds that had been gathering overhead since noon only added to his gloom. The clock chimed five and the first few drops began to fall, the swollen clouds no longer able to contain their heavy burden. If only, thought Adam, gazing sickly at the sky, I could unload my conscience as easily.

His face was getting wet as he stood at the open window and, as he reached up to wipe the rain away from his eyes, he noticed Lyon and LeLièvre walking down the road towards the river and the edge of town. He was suddenly galvanized into action.

"I'll follow them," he rationalized, "and make sure that no one comes to harm." With a feeling of relief that he had finally made a decision, Adam picked up his coat from the peg behind the door and set off to follow his friends. He was careful to remain a discreet distance back but almost lost his nerve when he saw Lyon and LeLièvre take a detour about a hundred yards from the Tay River. With sober countenances and unfaltering step, the two young men turned to the right and walked into the burying ground.

❧

The clock was striking the hour and James Boulton was disturbed from his concentration by the cool wind that brushed his neck. Shivering, he looked up and noticed that rain was coming in the open window. As he rose to shut the window, the door to his office burst open and his client James Hubbell exploded into the room.

"Boulton, you've got to stop them!"

Papers, caught in the tempest, blew every which way. Boulton spun around and reached out wildly to catch his disturbed work.

"Stop who, James. And what do you think you're doing storming in here like this?"

"Wilson and Robertson, that's who," Hubbell gasped. "They're meeting Lyon and LeLièvre on the banks of the Tay at Powell's farm."

"It's raining, Hubbell. Why would anyone want to meet anybody down by the river in weather like this?"

"It's not a bloody picnic, Boulton," exploded the panicked and exasperated Hubbell. "They're duelling, and as Wilson is your employee, I feel that it is your duty to stop him."

"Calm down, Hubbell. Wilson already knows my opinion in this matter. He's not going to do anything foolish, and besides, I'm not about to risk my death by going out there to repeat myself."

"It's not your death I'm worried about, Boulton," pressed Hubbell more urgently. "This is serious. We don't have a minute to lose. Now where is your coat?" He looked frantically behind the door.

"It's at the house. I didn't wear one today as I didn't expect it to rain."

"We don't have time to get it now." Hubbell grabbed Boulton by the arm and quick marched him out the door. "We've got to stop them before it's too late."

The dampness made the ashes heavy, but William Reade, a sturdy lad of about thirteen, was determined to finish this batch of potash before it got too dark. A shadow crossed the doorway, obliterating what little light remained. William looked up to make a sharp comment and saw that it was the deputy sheriff, Alexander Powell, and George Lyon.

"Laddie, have you seen two men come by?" asked Powell.

"Aye," he replied, "and noo too long ago."

"What did they look like?" asked Lyon.

"Well, one had on a cloak . . ."

"That's them," interrupted Lyon and the two men were gone as quickly as they came.

William looked out the door as the two men ran into the rain. They stopped to talk to two other men who were heading in the same direction and then advanced along the river bank together. William shook his head and returned to his work thinking that whatever was the matter, it wasn't his problem. He had nearly forgotten all about the interruption when he heard a gun shot. He remembered some rumours that had been flying around town that day, and dropping his shovel, he ran to the house for an umbrella and followed the route he had seen the men take.

Dr William Hamilton, surgeon to the First Lanark Militia for less than a year, hunched his shoulders to squelch the rain's passage down his neck. The two seconds, Simon Fraser Robertson and Henri LeLièvre, were examining the weapons before loading. If they don't hurry up, he thought hopefully, the powder will be too wet to fire.

"Gentlemen?"

"Everything is in order, Dr Hamilton," remarked LeLièvre as he cocked the hammer into place.

"Fine. Mr Wilson? Mr Lyon? Will you come forward and take your places, please."

The two combatants collected the weapons from their seconds and paced off to Dr Hamilton's count. They turned and fired.

The explosion was deafening as the two pistols fired almost simultaneously. Smoke briefly enveloped the two young men, obliterating them from each other's view, and then was washed away by the rain.

The two remained standing. Wilson's arm collapsed to his side, unable to bear the weight of the awkward weapon any longer. His arm shook, and he tried to keep the tremor from spreading to the rest of his body. He had no idea where his bullet had gone to. He only knew that he was still alive. And Lyon was still alive. Simon came up to him, retrieved the pistol and patted him gently on the shoulder. Relieved of its burden, his hand sprang up to touch the lock of hair that had been brushed by Lyon's bullet.

"Will the seconds please come forward?" LeLièvre and Robertson walked over to where Dr Hamilton was standing and presented the weapons for his inspection.

"Everything appears to be in order, gentlemen," he remarked casually. "Now, I think that it would be in everyone's best interest if we took a few minutes to reflect and then, perhaps, seek a reconciliation? Mr Wilson and Mr Lyon have conducted themselves well here this evening, and I think that it is safe to say that honour on both sides has been satisfied."

"Ah, but that is where you are wrong, my good doctor." Robertson and Hamilton looked at LeLièvre in astonishment. "Honour has yet to be satisfied this evening."

"Whatever can you mean, man?" exploded Robertson before the impervious LeLièvre. "We have conducted ourselves according to the Code.[1] Shots have been exchanged . . ."

"I'm going to speak to Lyon," interrupted Dr Hamilton.

Dr Hamilton paced across the sodden grass to where Lyon was patiently watching some ducks who had cautiously returned to feed along the river bank.

[1] The Duelling Code, which was followed in substance by the English-speaking world for almost a century, was settled by the Gentlemen Delegates of Tipperary, Galway, Mayo, Sligo and Roscommon at the Clonmel Assizes in 1775. It laid out the particulars for proper duelling by gentlemen.

"LeLièvre wants to continue," he said, interrupting Lyon's reverie. "For God's sake, Lyon, is there no way to put a stop to this unfortunate business?"

"Doctor, it is impossible," replied Lyon. "You know as well as I do that the Duelling Code states that when one man gives the other the lie and then that man retorts by a blow, no reconciliation can take place until after two discharges each, or a severe hit."

"We have not had a hit, Dr Hamilton," observed LeLièvre coolly. The Frenchman had silently appeared at the surgeon's side.

Dr Hamilton opened his mouth as if to argue the point, then, realizing the futility of it, clamped it shut and strode off to where Wilson and Robertson were waiting.

"Are they agreeable to a reconciliation, Dr Hamilton?" asked Robertson, barely able to contain his agitation.

"No."

"We are prepared to meet them halfway," offered Robertson. "In fact, we are quite anxious that this matter be brought to a peaceful conclusion."

"I'll try again."

However, before Dr Hamilton could take more than two steps in Lyon's direction, he noticed that the young man was pointing the pistol towards him.

The four men stood on a rise about a quarter of a mile from where the duel was taking place.

"Can you tell who is who?" asked Boulton.

"No," replied Powell. "It's raining too hard to distinguish them. George, do you think we should go and interfere?"

"No. There doesn't appear to be any harm done. Christ, this weather is enough to dampen the most rabid hothead."

"Well," remarked Boulton as he sat down on a fallen log, "I can at least be comfortable." Hubbell looked dourly down at him as the rain poured off the brim of his hat onto Boulton's shoe. "Relatively speaking. Hey, who's that young lad? Should he be here?"

William Reade was struggling along the cow path beside the river, dwarfed by the umbrella he was carrying.

"Reade, isn't it?" demanded Hubbell. "What are you doing here? Shouldn't you be minding your father's potash works?"

"Tis milking time, sir," panted William. "I've come to round up the cows. Kinna help y' sirs?"

"Oh, we're just looking for some people . . ."

Suddenly, there was a massive flash of lightning, as if Zeus himself had fired the bolt to earth with all his might. The thunder applauded the display, and a pistol shot rang out in defiance of the forces of nature.

The two seconds met again to inspect the weapons under the supervision of Dr Hamilton. No one said a word. Robertson briskly examined both pistols and nodded his curt acceptance to the surgeon. LeLièvre scanned them as carelessly as if he were selecting an inexpensive bauble for a lady friend.

When both men declared themselves satisfied, Dr Hamilton again called the principals forward to select their weapons. With quick, efficient movements, Lyon presented himself and chose the pistol closest to him. Wilson had to be prompted by his second to approach the surgeon, and finally, Simon Fraser Robertson thrust the pistol into his cold hands.

It was drizzling steadily now and the damp struck cold to the bone. The principals' boots made gasping, sucking noises, and left gaping wounds in the mud of the freshly ploughed field, as they paced off the distance to their places.

Despite the confidence that he displayed, Lyon was in no way feeling sure of his ability to survive, unharmed, another exchange. He remembered the dream he had had, twice in the past fortnight. He dreamt that he had walked past the burying grounds dressed in his grave clothes. His face relaxed into a quick smile as he recalled his landlady's horrified expression at such a blasphemy. He gave himself a mental shake. He was a crack shot, he chided himself, and Wilson was just a bumbling farm boy. Why, he'd managed to discompose the upstart by brushing the side of his temple during the last exchange.

Lyon positioned himself in the middle of the furrow where LeLièvre had indicated he should stand. The rain made it difficult for him to see clearly, and he couldn't keep his hands dry, but the furrow gave him a direct line to Wilson's heart.

Wilson saw where Lyon stood and saw him raise his pistol in a direct line with his body. I shall fall, he thought, surprised he was so dispassionate. He felt the coldness of his actions. It was time. The most horrific bolt of lightning rent the skies, illuminating all who stood defiantly below.

Wilson turned his head away and fired.

All the spectators raced to the downed man.

Dr Hamilton crouched by Robert Lyon, who lay where he had fallen. Wilson's bullet had entered the right side of his chest. Hamilton tried to staunch the blood washing over Lyon's white linen shirt but, when he noticed it was also bubbling at his mouth, he knew that Lyon's lung had been perforated. Minutes later, Robert Lyon, aged nineteen, was dead.

Epilogue

John Wilson and Simon Fraser Robertson immediately surrendered themselves to the authorities. They stood trial in Brockville that August, as the duel had taken place over the town line in the District of Johnstown, and acted as their own defence under the counsel of Henry Sherwood. Sherwood later rose to prominence as Solicitor-General (1842) and Attorney-General (1847) for Canada West.

Wilson and Robertson were found not guilty by the jury. General feeling had it that they were let off because the jury was Irish and the Irish "consider fighting commendable, rather than a crime."[2]

At the end of October, James Boulton left Perth for Niagara, most likely for his own safety. Thomas Radenhurst, Lyon's employer, had, in a drunken rage, run through Boulton's home with a pistol the day after the duel. Neither was Boulton missed by the third lawyer in town, Daniel McMartin. On the day Boulton departed, McMartin:

---

[2] Rev. Wm. Bell Diaries, 10 August 1833.

. . . proposed to have bonfires and other signs of rejoicing. After seven in the evening I heard a stir in the streets and horns blowing as for a charivari. Soon after a cavalcade appeared, attended by a crowd of boys and other idle people. In the middle was a waggon, bearing a gibbet from which hung a figure representing Mr. Boulton with a large paper lantern and light in front, to render the whole invisible. After parading through the principal street, they burnt the figure . . . not however without opposition from his well-wishers who put out the fire and scattered the actors . . . [3]

Wilson eventually followed Boulton to Niagara, after closing down the Perth practice. He had a successful career, both before the bar and on the bench, and eventually became the Member of Parliament for London (1847) and a member of the Supreme Court of Ontario.

His understanding with Joanna Lees was broken off immediately by her parents, despite several attempts made by him to explain and rectify matters with her. His unrequited infatuation for Elizabeth Hughes was dead. However, in the spring of 1835, he did offer for and marry Miss Hughes, who had been reduced to even more straightened circumstances due to her connection with the fatal duel. This marriage of convenience appeased Wilson's sense of honour. He believed himself the cause of Elizabeth Hughes' social ruin and marriage to him would save her from a life of probable destitution. They had three children, and Justice Wilson died on the third of June, 1869, a respected and revered man. Mrs Wilson lived until 1904 and died at the age of ninety-three.

Henri LeLièvre, considered by many to be the real culprit in this affair, fled Perth immediately following the duel and never stood trial for his part in the affair. He eventually made his way to Australia where he ended his days.

Robert Lyon was buried in the Radenhurst family plot, in the same burying ground that he passed through on his way to the duelling site. His gravestone still stands and is inscribed:

[3] Ibid. October 1833.

Friendship Offering
Dedicated
To the Memory of
ROBERT LYON
(Student-at-Law)
He fell
in mortal combat
13th of June, 1833
in the 20th year of his age.
Requiescat in
Pace.

Silhouettes of John Wilson and Robert Lyon.
Perth Museum Collection.

Brockville, Nov. 14th, 1832.   46

ADVERTISEMENT.

TERMS of Mrs. Acland's SEMINARY for Young Ladies, Perth, Upper-Canada.

Junior Pupils, Reading, Writing and Needlework, } per ann.	£3	0	0
General instruction, including English Grammar, Exercises and composition, Geography, with the use of the Globes, Ancient and Modern History Writing, Arithmetic and Needlework	5	0	0
French,	4	0	0
Italian,	4	0	0
Music,	7	0	0
Use of Pianoforte,	1	0	0
Drawing,	5	0	0
Dancing,	4	0	0
Board,	25	0	0
Fuel during winter,	0	10	0
Use of Books for English Reading,	0	10	0
Washing,	2	10	0

Boarders are required to provide their own beds, bedding, towels, desert and teaspoon. Any articles sent for the accommodation of the pupils will be returned on their removal from the school:—No pupil will be received for less than a quarter; and a month's notice will be expected previous to their leaving the school. Two Vacations of a fortnight each will be allowed in the course of the year, which will be considered a part of the quarters in which they occur. Accounts to be settled quarterly. Mrs. Acland will be prepared to receive a few boarders on the first of July next.

In conducting this establishment Mrs. Acland hopes by the greatest attention on her part to the improvement and domestic comfort of her pupils, to merit the approbation of those parents who may favour her with their patronage.

Perth, 30th May, 1831   23u

Advertisement for Mrs Ackland's Seminary for Young Ladies, *Brockville Recorder,* May 1834.

The Summit House, Drummond Street East. Built in the then-fashionable Adamesque style in 1823 by James Boulton, the Summit House was modelled after The Grange, home of the influential Boulton family in York (Toronto). This grand home was one of the few in the Rideau Corridor to be built of brick at this early date—the readily available wood and stone being more popular materials. Soon after the Wilson-Lyon duel, Boulton was burned in effigy on the front lawn. This prompted him to put the Summit House up for sale and move to Niagara.
Credit: Greg Anderson

Inge-Va, 66 Craig Street. The Reverend Michael Harris built this classic Colonial Georgian house in 1824, but by 1832, it was the home of Thomas Radenhurst. Robert Lyon's body was brought here after his duel with Wilson. Recognized as a fine example of the Ontario Cottage, this modestly sized home has five fireplaces, each with a differently designed Adam mantel. It was named Inge-Va (Tamil for come here) by the third owners, the Inderwicks, who had lived in Ceylon.
Credit: Stephanie Strachan

Pistols used by John Wilson and Robert Lyon. Perth Museum Collection.
Credit: Kim Rennick.

BIBLIOGRAPHY

PRIMARY SOURCES

Archives of Ontario.

Bathurst Courier. Algonquin College, Perth Campus.

The Brockville Recorder. Algonquin College, Perth Campus.

The Bathurst Independent Examiner. Perth Museum.

Diaries of the Rev. William Bell. Perth Museum.

Papers of the Perth Historical & Antiquarian Society. Perth, Ontario, 1896. Perth Museum.

Perth Museum Archives.

Public Archives of Canada.

The Perth Courier. Algonquin College, Perth Campus.

Rideau Canal Archives.

Tay Navigation Company Ledger, 13 May 1834—17 November 1835. Private Collection.

SECONDARY SOURCES

Bell, Rev. William. *Hints to Emigrants.* Edinburgh, 1824.

Brown, Howard Morton. *Lanark Legacy—Nineteenth Century Glimpses of an Ontario County.* County of Lanark, 1984.

Brown, Jack. *Olden Days at Playfairville.* 1972.

Byron, George Gordon, Lord. "Childe Harold's Pilgrimage, Canto III," *The Norton Anthology of English Literature,* Volume 2. W.W. Norton & Company, New York. Fourth Edition. 1979.

Craig, Gerald M. *Upper Canada The Formative Years, 1784-1841*. McClelland and Stewart Limited, Toronto. 1991.

Gourlay, Robert. *Statistical Account of Upper Canada*. London, 1822.

Kennedy, James R. *South Elmsley in the Making 1783-1983*. Township of South Elmsley & James R. Kennedy. 1984.

McGill, Jean S. *Pioneer History of the County of Lanark*. Clay Publishing Company, 1979.

McNaught, Kenneth. *The Pelican History of Canada*. Penguin Books, Markham. 1978.

Morgan, H.R. "The First Tay Canal." *Ontario Historical Society Papers*, Volume 29. 1933.

Shortt, Edward. *The Memorable Duel at Perth*. The Perth Museum, Perth. 1970.

Shortt, Edward (ed.). *Perth Remembered*. The Perth Museum, Perth. 1967.

Taylor, Michael. *Perth's First Murder, in 1828, was a Grisly One*. The Perth Courier. 25 June 1986.

Tomalin, Claire. *Mrs Jordan's Profession: The Actress and the Prince*. Alfred A. Knopf, New York. 1995.

Turner, Larry. *The First Tay Canal in the Rideau Corridor 1830-1850*. Parks Canada, 1984.

Turner, Larry. *Perth, Tradition & Style in Eastern Ontario*. Natural Heritage, Toronto. 1992.

Turner, Larry. *The "Shinplasters" of W. & J. Bell, Perth, Upper Canada, 1837-1839*. Perth Museum Archives. 1985.

Walker, Harry & Olive. *Carleton Saga*. Harry Walker. 1968.

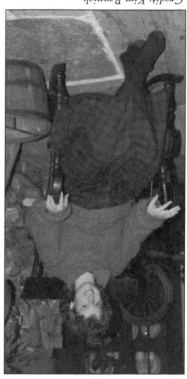

ABOUT THE AUTHOR

Susan Code was born and still lives in Perth, Ontario, and has been fascinated with and telling stories about the area since she was a child. She has pursued a variety of career paths—including historical interpreter, copy writer and assistant to a Member of Parliament—but for several years now has abandoned financial security to freelance as a writer and editor.

Although she holds an honours degree in history from Queen's University at Kingston, she still cannot explain the Whig interpretation of history, preferring instead to embrace the subject as something to be seen, heard, smelled, tasted and touched.

Credit: Kim Rennick

To order more copies of

A

MATTER

OF

HONOUR

send $18.95 plus $4.50 to cover
GST, shipping and handling to:
GENERAL STORE PUBLISHING HOUSE
1 Main Street, Burnstown, Ontario
K0J 1G0

Telephone: 1-800-465-6072
Fax: 613-432-7184